COMMON GROUND

Where the mind cannot see order, it sees chaos. Chaos is always giving way to order as knowledge and insight develop.

—Howard W. Thurman

The power of the oppressor lies in the submission of the people. When black people really unite and rise up in all their splendid millions, they will have the strength to smash injustice.

—Huey P. Newton

COMMON GROUND

A COMPARISON OF THE IDEAS OF CONSCIOUSNESS IN THE WRITINGS OF HOWARD W. THURMAN AND HUEY P. NEWTON

Anthony Sean Neal

AFRICA WORLD PRESS
541 West Ingham Avenue | Suite B
Trenton, New Jersey 08638

Book and Cover Design: SpiralUp Solutions (P) Ltd.
Cover Photo of Hugh P. Newton: Gary Freedman/With Permission of Camera Press Ltd.
Cover Photo of Howard T. Thurman: With Permission of Boston University, buphotos.

Library of Congress Cataloging in Publication Data

Neal, Anthony Sean.
Common ground: a comparison of the ideas of consciousness in the writings of Howard W. Thurman and Huey P. Newton / Anthony Sean Neal.
    pages cm
Includes bibliographical references and index.
    ISBN978-1-59221-996-4(hardcover)--ISBN978-1-59221-997-1(pbk.)
1. Thurman, Howard, 1900-1981. 2. Newton, Huey P. 3. Consciousness.
4. Liberty. 5. Community development. I. Title.
BX6495.T53N43 2015
305.896'073--dc23
                                    2014045332

CONTENTS

ACKNOWLEDGMENTS

I would like to thank Dr. Charles Duncan, Dr. Daniel Black, Dr. Fragano Ledgister, and Dr. Luther Smith for their direction, assistance, and guidance. In particular, Dr. Duncan's recommendations and suggestions have been invaluable for this research.

I would like to thank the students of the Department of African American Studies, Dr. Josephine Bradley, and Dr. Daniel Black whose conversations and critiques helped to focus my topic in its beginning. I am also thankful to Dr. Barrow and Dr. Osinubi for their leadership of the doctoral program.

Special thanks go to my parents, Tom and Mary Frances Neal Jr., who gave me their last to ensure my success. My children and my brother have also been indispensable. Finally, words alone cannot express the thanks I owe to Willette Neal, my wife, for her encouragement and assistance.

PREFACE

In my undergraduate years at Morehouse College, I was introduced to the writings of Howard Thurman, an esteemed alumnus of the college. I was captivated by his ability to always seek an experience with the Holy despite his lived experience. Thurman also had a strong desire to create a community of individuals focused on creating the desired experience of encountering the Holy. It became clear to me that Thurman believed community was a necessary component toward the goal of realizing this desired experience, which, for Thurman, represented the ultimate freedom. During this time, I began to quote Thurman along with many other philosophers such as Rawls and Dewey, when debating the necessary steps to better the black community, especially in inner cities.

In one of these campus debates, I was challenged by another student who asked whether I had considered Huey P. Newton's idea of intercommunalism while deliberating this subject. I was ashamed to admit that I had not even known that he had written books. Almost at once, I began reading Newton's works searching for anything worthy of consideration. It was during this period that I discovered that although Newton and Thurman were miles apart in method, they were addressing the same questions and arriving at very similar conclusions. In fact, their writings suggest that both Newton and Thurman believed a community focused on the same goals could solve many social problems, creating space for the desired experience of freedom to blossom. Most importantly, they both believed that to create this type of community, the members would have to experience a transformation of consciousness. It became my desire to understand how two individuals who were so different came to such similar conclusions, even writing books with very similar titles dedicated mostly to this topic.

It was in a graduate seminar that the answer to this question became clear. After becoming immersed in the writings of many black social thinkers, an almost undetectable common thread appeared, which was a focus on the idea of consciousness and its effect on the nature of the black community. The occasion for this investigation, then, was a desire to understand the usage of the idea of consciousness as a phenomenon in black culture and what effect, if any, the African aesthetic transposed by the desire for freedom had on this phenomenon.

There seemed to be some commonality of ideas developing within the black intellectual tradition and it is my intention to identify any confluence of thought and develop an explanation for the existence of any identified confluence. This will be done by choosing two prominent African American shapers of culture from the modern era of African American studies (from the conferring of the PhD on W. E. B. Du Bois to the end of the Vietnam War in 1975) and examining their work through the prism of the African (Freedom) aesthetic. The two scholars to be examined are Howard W. Thurman and Huey P. Newton. There were many African American writers from the examination period who exhibited similarities in their writings concerning community development and social transformation, but Howard Thurman and Huey Newton were chosen because the similarities in their writings led me to form questions concerning the confluence in their ideas. The purpose of this research is to show the existence of the confluence and to use the African (Freedom) aesthetic as framework for the creation of an answer to why this phenomenon exists.

INTRODUCTION

STATEMENT OF THE PROBLEM

This book will compare and interpret the idea of consciousness in the writings of Huey Percy Newton and Howard Washington Thurman. Each man's idea of consciousness was built on seemingly opposing schools of thought; however, there is confluence in their usage of consciousness as the driving force of their strategies for community development and social transformation. In this study, it will be shown that this confluence was a result of their shared cultural aesthetic created by the experience of being African American in the modern era.[1] The use of the term consciousness to describe a particular phenomenon manifested by two individuals separated by such a generational gap is significant, especially when considering the fact that the only connection they share is a cultural experience fertilized by the existence of racial oppression. Consciousness, in this sense, is a term that is frequently used in the African American linguistic vernacular. Consciousness is defined as the awareness of a mental event or phenomenal reality that can be realized or understood, and as it applies to this research, the mental event or phenomenal reality to be understood is "being black." This can also be understood variously as blackness (the color), black existence, or black beingness. In this usage, it is understood that a shared understanding of what it means to be black constitutes a transpersonal collective consciousness. To this point, it has taken on a cultural meaning that can be identified by certain cultural phenomena, such as conscious rap, conscious art, or black consciousness.

However, with all the conversation centered on the concept of consciousness, the definition has often been assumed. In the African

American vernacular, very less attention has been given to the usage of consciousness as an aesthetic phenomenon and to the development of the concept over time, while even less has been given to the origin of its usage in black culture. For this reason, it is necessary to examine consciousness as a linguistic phenomenon to provide the foundation from which to explore its special significance for Thurman and Newton. Often the words "conscious" and "consciousness" are used synonymously; however, the state of being conscious refers to the acquired and sustained physiological and psychological alertness that allows the conscious being to have knowledge of, to recall and recollect both "past and contemporary, internal and external events"; to intentionally focus on specific phenomena; and to choose certain interactions with the environment in which to participate with others for the furthering of personal goals. This state is what many simply refer to as wakefulness or knowingness. Consciousness, however, can be understood as knowledge of a specific phenomenal reality. It means literally "with knowledge," and to the extent that intelligence is related to knowledge, the concepts are fundamentally related. Simply put, consciousness is awareness intentionally focused on a physical object or mental creation that is subjectively understood. It can also be understood as a state of mind that, in the case of groups bonded by shared experience, constitutes a transpersonal collective consciousness. It is worth noting that also associated with consciousness are varying degrees of awareness that give way to enabling or hindering the ability of the individual to participate in certain types of mental and behavioral activities. When people enter into a particular state of consciousness, they are in effect transformed. This is due to the multiple manifestations of behavior, which become concretized into practices and are said to portray perceptions, ways of thinking, or cultural affirmations. So then, to change consciousness is to change the mental attributes of an individual or community.

When considering the change in the perception of a community, causal relationships provide a point from which to begin an archaeological study to determine an explanation for the direction of the shift in perception. An archaeological study is a study involving historical digs of information along with linguistic analysis and interpretation of ideological meaning. With the ultimate objective of this study in mind, the origins of consciousness as an aesthetic phenomenon in the African American vernacular is focused on in the following section.

Since its beginning, the collective consciousness of the African American community has been uniquely shaped and altered by its leaders. Black leadership in America was an outgrowth of the circumstances in which blacks found themselves as a result of the oppressive conditions brought about by slavery; however, this leadership was nurtured and became systematic within the framework of the black church and black religious movements. This is well documented by writers such as Gayraud Wilmore, Henry J. Young, Albert J. Raboteau, and Carter G. Woodson. In Young's work on major black religious leaders, he notes the efforts of these early leaders to transform the consciousness of enslaved blacks. Quoting Philip A. Bruce in his work on *Black Religion and Black Radicalism*, Gayraud Wilmore states,

> The preacher of the negroes are their most active politicians, as a rule, but even when they are not they have many political influences, for they constitute, individually, the natural leaders of their race, being elevated to their clerical position not because they are men of greater holiness of life or eloquence of tongue than the rest of their fellows, but because they have more energy and decision of character.[2]

Their energy and decision of character can be equated to their concept of consciousness. It was this consciousness that allowed these leaders to desire an experience that was over and beyond their lived experience of oppression. These leaders made use of a religious framework that was focused on the lifting or changing of consciousness. The use of a religious framework also made the idea of consciousness transformation a natural development in African American culture.

Although many religious leaders worked desperately to change black consciousness or the black perception of self, the most prominent of the group is W. E. B. Du Bois, who, in *The Souls of Black Folk*, famously described the Negro (black) understanding of self as being a "double consciousness." Dr Du Bois arrived at this conclusion through his perception of black experience. This observation leads him to ask the question, "How does it feel to be a problem," which he uses as a premise throughout the book to interpret the black experience. The definition of the double consciousness, to view one's self through another's eyes, set in motion many years of discussion centered around what exactly is the nature of the black experience.

As a graduate student, Du Bois traveled to the University of Berlin to study with Max Weber. Under Weber, Du Bois learned a tradition of sociology heavily rooted in the teachings of Karl Marx. In fact, Karl Marx's explication of class consciousness has served as the foundation for much of the social and political philosophy that developed among African Americans. This is demonstrated in writings that use Marx as the foundational source to build an African Diaspora system of social reflective thought in the modern era. Aimé Césaire, Léopold Senghor, Franz Fanon, and Kwame Nkrumah (who was educated in the United States at a historically black college) all have a social component to their writings that is clearly predicated on Marxist thought. These writings also served as an impetus to the political theory of Huey Newton.

The connection of Howard Thurman's thoughts to Marxist philosophy is less documented in literature. Thurman attended Rochester Theological Seminary, which was the center of the Social Gospel. The Social Gospel was the twentieth century movement among protestant theologians that stressed the need to apply Christian principles to society's problems. It is thought to be based on the teachings of a German immigrant theologian named Walter Rauschenbusch. While at Rochester, Thurman studied under George Cross, who was a colleague and mentee of Walter Rauschenbusch, also referred to as the father of the Social Gospel. Rauschenbusch studied in Germany for four years, where he studied the writings of Karl Marx and other social thinkers. From their thoughts, he developed the Social Gospel. Thus, Thurman's connection to Marx is through Cross's connection to the unquestionably Marxist Rauschenbusch.

Huey Newton's induction into Marxist thought takes a different course. Newton's collegiate education took place during a period when Marx's writings became a major source of inspiration for those interested in transforming the oppressive conditions under which blacks lived in the United States and abroad. While a student at Merritt College, Newton read writings by Marx and developed much of the Black Panther philosophy based on these writings. Newton even referred to himself as a dialectical materialist, claiming that he was attempting to mobilize the *lumpenproletariat*, not the educated working class like Marx. He chose the Marxist signifier *lumpenproletariat* because of the material conditions of the average black in America. He wrote that the purpose of establishing the Black Panther Party was to raise the consciousness of the people. Newton believed, like Marx, that making people aware of the causes of the contradictions in the society gave them the power to defend themselves from the elements that hindered good life.

In this study, significant attention will be given to both Thurman's and Newton's usage of the idea of consciousness in forming their conception of community development and social transformation. The information gathered will be used to determine the extent to which a common ground exists in the writings of these two intellectuals. Interestingly, in 1971, both men were pondering the question of the true essence of community and wrote books with similar titles in which they engaged in a virtual dialogue on this very subject.[3] Although they were not actually conversing with each other, they did in fact arrive at similar points of view on this important topic. After explicating the need for community, they focused their discussions on what each of them considered as the essence of community. Consciousness, by absentee conversation, is agreed on by both men as the common force on which community must be built. Each man, in his own way, from his own experience, focused on the processes that caused communities to form. Each man's quest began because of his earnest desire to find the solution(s) to the human problems caused by the hegemonic domination of one race by another. Newton's book was co-written with Erik Erikson, a well-known professor of psychoanalytical thought and human development. While Newton asserted in his book that the primary concern of the Black Panther Party was to lift the consciousness of the people, his understanding of consciousness, and its role in community development, shows a progressive line of development in his writings. Thurman follows a similar line of thought, although Thurman's progress is over a much longer expanse of time. In his book, in response to the division of the nation because of the death of Martin Luther King, Jr.,[4] Thurman writes that he believed the Black Power ideologues misunderstood that at the basic nature of the human being, there is a desire to be in a community. This lack of understanding, according to Thurman, hindered their desire for true social consciousness. Thurman explains that the paradox of conscious life is the ultimate focus of his book, as explicit in the title of the book, *The Search for Common Ground.*

It is the aim of this writer to compare and evaluate each of these authors' understanding of consciousness as a unique African American social construct. This topic was chosen for several reasons, the most prominent of which is the fact that both men had an enormous effect on African American thought during the civil rights movement and both men continue to have significant influence today, although neither is studied much in the world of academia. However, the efforts of these men in changing the perception of the society has had an impact on a number of people, which is enough in itself to make them worthy of study.

Howard Thurman, although the lesser known among the two, has written over twenty books. After serving as professor of religion at both Morehouse and Spelman colleges, he became the Dean of Rankin Chapel at the Howard University and then went on to become the first black to be a dean at a major university (Boston University). He co-founded the first interfaith/interracial church in the United States. He mentored many civil rights leaders, most notably Martin Luther King, who is said to have carried a copy of Thurman's book in his briefcase while traveling. Huey Newton, besides co-founding the Black Panther Party, authored five books. Countless men and women were influenced by Newton, and many programs that he began were later adopted by the government (such as free lunch and head-start). Most of all, he taught blacks that the true essence of revolution is a function of social consciousness.

PURPOSE OF THE STUDY

The purpose of this study is to explicate and compare the ideas of consciousness in the writings of Huey P. Newton and Howard W. Thurman. A secondary aim is to identify confluence in their ideas and to explain the reasons for the confluence. Consciousness as a concept has been mentioned in other writings concerning Howard W. Thurman and Huey P. Newton; however, there has been no investigative attempt to understand consciousness as the foundational concept of their ideas nor does the literature suggest evidence of any comparative analysis of the thought of these two men The fact that Howard Thurman's and Huey Newton's ideas develop from divergent sources makes this task difficult. Thus, an inquiry of this sort is needed because it provides a conceptual framework within which to situate the works of African American social thinkers from the modern era.

Black social thinkers have not done well in the area of connecting their thoughts to the thoughts of other black thinkers when it comes to the topic of consciousness and its connection to community development/social transformation. Much of the problem can be attributed to the overt attempts to connect this black scholarship to the Western mainstream academic scholars. This disconnect among black scholars has created a lacuna in the analysis of their works for the existence of confluence concerning the idea of consciousness. Wade Nobles[5] is one among the few scholars who have attempted to create a work that utilizes mostly black scholarly sources to fully explain consciousness as it pertains to community development/social transformation.

It is the author's intent to develop a theory to explain how the cultural aesthetic of Thurman and Newton shaped their thought causing confluence in their theories of community development/ social transformation. A literature search showed that no other studies have attempted to use a cultural aesthetic to analyze and explain the existence of confluence in theories of community development/social transformation among African Americans. This book will also be useful as a basis for the identification of common lines of thought in the writings of other African American social thinkers from the modern era.

PREVIOUS RESEARCH

Previous research on Newton or Thurman has not focused specifically on their idea of consciousness. However, a number of researchers have discussed their ideas of consciousness but only so that other concepts could be more fully understood. Luther Smith and Walter Fluker have both done biographical analyses of Thurman. Smith's work on Thurman also includes a critical evaluation of Thurman's work, in which he defines the style of Thurman's mysticism as prophetic.[6] Fluker's writings concerning Thurman describe the technique Thurman uses, which he refers to as social mysticism, to develop his ethical critique of society through his connection to the black church.[7]

Dissertations on Thurman have been written by Carlyle Fielding Stewart, Mozella Mitchell, and Ivory Lyons. While Stewart's work centers on Thurman's ethical ontology,[8] Mitchell wrestles with Thurman's concept of conversion[9] and Lyons discusses Thurman's concept of sin and justice.[10] Each of these writings is valuable in itself; however, more importantly, they demonstrate how to systematically study a non-systematic thinker.

In 1969, James H. Cone authored the monumental theological work, *Black Theology and Black Power*.[11] This work was one of the first scholarly attempts to identify the connection between black religious thought and black radical thought using systematic theology. In this work, Cone equates spirit with black political consciousness. This type of consciousness, according to Cone, seeks to meet the needs of the oppressed. It is at this juncture that Black Power "soul" meets the soul of Black Religion. Cone puts forth the idea that Black Power and Black Religion are both focused on the liberation of black people and come together in Black Liberation Theology.

Gayraud Wilmore pursues this thread further in *Black Religion and Black Radicalism*.[12] This book, which was dedicated to analyzing the development of black religion in America from the period of slavery to the period of civil rights during the 1960s, argues that the African spiritual tradition and the radical nature of black politics that was developed through the experience of slavery and oppression were fused together to form the salient features of the black religion. Wilmore explained that it was from this frame of reference that the black experience was interpreted by the black community at large until the demise of the black power era in the late 1970s.

Leonard E. Barrett's book, *Soul-Force*, directs attention toward the development and existence of the black freedom aesthetic.[13] Due to the black man's original position in the Americas as slave and his subsequently low social position, the black man has had to fight his way up in this land of his exile. But as he fights, he proves that his soul-force (consciousness) is not just a passive means of survival, but an active instrument of culture formation. This book makes use of the idea of consciousness that Barrett calls soul-force, the spiritual energy that brought our ancestors through the long struggle in servitude, and that continued to shape the lives of black people through the 1970s.

Mark Anthony Neal continues with the thought of a soul-(force) aesthetic, by using this line of reasoning to develop his concept of the post-soul aesthetic.[14] In his book, *Soul Babies: Black Popular Culture and the Post-Soul Aesthetic*, Neal advances the idea that prior to 1978, black America had developed a unique aesthetic, which he terms the "soul aesthetic," but since 1978, black American ideas have been shaped by what he calls the post-soul aesthetic. Neal explains the post-soul aesthetic by putting forth the concept that blacks, in their attempt to become fully American, experienced contradictions that initiated a distinctive black post- modernity, characterized by a marriage of the ideas of protest to the culture of middle-income college-educated young adults who had neither lived through the civil rights movement nor knew of its struggles.

In *Black Power Ideologies*, John T. McCartney comments on the sources of Newton's idea of consciousness and also describes the methodology Newton used to create his political theory.[15] According to McCartney, Newton believed that the church as well as the Black Panthers had a responsibility to make people aware of the obstacles that oppressed them. Although McCartney's book is useful, it does not give extensive consideration to what exactly Newton's definition is and how consciousness shapes his thought.

Erik Erikson joined Newton to present in their book a series of conversations designed to find points of contact through which to analyze each other's ideology.[16] *The Search for Common Ground* is very profound in that it presents Erikson's critique of Newton's theories while in real-time conversation with the latter. Erikson's sincere attempt to understand Newton's theories adds value to the conversation because it is by far almost the only such attempt by any non-African American.

In *Seize the Time*, Bobby Seale apologetically introduces the means by which the theory of consciousness, as expressed by Newton, was used to formulate the philosophical framework of the Black Panther Party in the form of the ten-point program.[17] It is in the application of this theory that Newton's methodological strategies concerning the manipulation of consciousness become exposed. This work identifies the raising of consciousness as the major thrust of Newton's theory of community development/social transformation.

RESEARCH QUESTIONS

The research questions that guide this study are as follows:

- What are the ideas of consciousness as represented in the writings of Howard Thurman and Huey Newton?
- How were their ideas of consciousness used to create a theory of community development/social transformation?
- Is there common ground or confluence in the ideas of these two scholars?

METHOD OF INQUIRY

Several methods of investigation will be used to complete this research. The author begins by looking at the thought of each man separately through the prism of the freedom aspect of the African aesthetic. The "freedom aspect" of the African aesthetic refers to how the perception of Africans developed as a result of their desire for freedom. After analyzing at the thought of each of these scholars separately, this research shall examine their ideas of consciousness to discover their convergent and divergent points. The author of this research also seeks to discover the form of the communal change Thurman and Newton envisioned as the outcome of heightened communal consciousness.

For the foundation of this analysis, the author uses categories created by Mirimba Ani (Dona Richards) in her concept of the African aesthetic, which she calls *Kugusa Mtima* (KM).[18] There are four categories of analysis described by Ani, which are transformation, transcendence, human consciousness, and the power of the collective human will. These categories will be used as a foundation for the formation of the conceptual framework and to explain how the experience of being a member of the diaspora has brought about a special phenomenon in the form of a modified aesthetic. KM means literally to touch the heart, and it attempts to reconnect emotion and thought when contemplating the idea of culture as it relates to Africans and the African diaspora. KM is the "African experience of being touched, moved, and affected by a self-consciously created experience or form/phenomenon."[19] KM outlines four categories in which these created experiences can be deciphered: transcendence, transformation, human consciousness, and the power of the collective will. KM will be used to explore the connection between the experience of being black, which will be referred to as variously blackness, the African aesthetic, or consciousness, depending on the particular context, as they are somewhat interchangeable terms. Along with KM, John Dewey's concept of aesthetic experience will be referenced as the foundation for the researcher's use of the term "aesthete" when referring to each subject and also to gain an understanding of how this particular nomenclature connects the personality of the two subjects with their concept of consciousness. According to Dewey, perception is an aesthetic experience to the degree that a form appears to the perceiver in the midst of multifaceted stimulus. Similarly, a lack of proper relationship and distribution, according to Dewey, causes confusion by blocking this singleness of perception. This concept is used also to critique the problems in the American society of his day. Dewey felt that lack of community in American cities in effect decreased the abilities of American citizens to actualize their full potential. Later in this study, an analogy is made between Dewey's concept of the perceiver/ aesthete and the ideas of consciousness in the writings of Thurman and Newton. Creating such an analogy will not only demonstrate points of contact but also produce significant points of departure by revealing that the particular usage of the idea of consciousness and the points of confluence found in the writings of Thurman and Newton arose from their specific cultural experiences.

It is this cultural experience that connects these two aesthetes and shapes the framework on which this study is built. The premise of this study is that the experience of blackness caused a strong desire for freedom in the consciousness of the Africans who were brought to the Americas. This consciousness gave rise to the occasion of the freedom movement. The existential reality of having to fight for freedom helped to create a modified form of the African aesthetic, which henceforth will be referred to as the African Freedom Aesthetic. However, this term is not to be thought of as synonymous with the aesthetic described by Addison Gayle and other writers of the black arts movement. Despite the similarities, the two major differences between the two understandings of aesthetics is that the aesthetic as described by Gayle is time locked as a phenomenon of the late 1960s and the early 1970s. It was also thought of as a corrective to the concept of the new negro movement created during the Harlem Renaissance. The African Freedom Aesthetic, however, had its beginning the moment the first African was put into captivity. It did not develop among only those who were considered to be the intelligentsia, but among all Africans who were held captive. It held on to many of the concepts from the African aesthetic but reshaped and refocused them to recognize the general desire for freedom that was common to all captive Africans. The major concepts that shape this aesthetic develop from the assumption that the experience of black oppression caused the development of several key concepts that have become a part of black rhetoric and the black thought structure. These concepts can be found in black humanistic expression from philosophy to fine art, and they form the conceptual framework of this study.

In the initial stages of this study, before the parameters were set concerning which works and writers would be examined, community development/social transformation and its causes were the foci of the research. As such, several African American social movements and social thinkers were studied to find the common causes of these movements. In the process of this examination, several interesting factors were noticed, with the common goal of freedom shared by all in some form. On this discovery, the author was forced to re-conceptualize the nature of how the movements would be understood. Instead of performing the study as if many movements had taken place, they would now be analyzed from the point of view that there was only one movement, the freedom movement, with many phases and one goal.

This discovery also made space for the study to focus on the ideological similarities that caused each phase and gave the momentum needed to create unity among the participants. The ideological facet of the study set the first parameter, which would be chronological. To have enough primary sources to study, the author focused on the modern era of African American studies because it was the first period when most black leaders were formally educated and produced writings concerning their ideas. This period dates from about 1896, which was the year W. E. B. Du Bois completed his dissertation, to 1975, the final year of troop withdrawal from Vietnam. These years were chosen as endpoints for this era primarily because Du Bois was the first academic to formally study African Americans, while the end of the Vietnam War brought about a new generation that had tasted a sense of equality through protest and fighting. The Vietnam War was the first war where blacks and whites fought side by side in the same foxholes since before the end of slavery. The recognition of the chronological connection gave this researcher the ability to reduce the ideas and exemplars being studied.

From this reduction, the author was able to form an ideological timeline based on the thinkers who played a major role in the perpetuation of ideas that enabled the continuation of the freedom movement. In 1903, W. E. B. Du Bois set out the intention of explaining the meaning of being black in the twentieth century. He defines blackness as a struggle that stems from being a problem. Du Bois goes further to say that the existential reality of blackness was the experience of double consciousness. This double consciousness is described by Du Bois as being at once Negro and American—a state of self-contradiction—which amounts to existential absurdity. However, he purports that the end of the absurdity was at hand, hastened by the recent emancipation of the Negro. He asserts that what was yet needed was a lifting of consciousness through an education aimed at community development/social transformation by striving for grander horizons. This set the stage for others to focus on consciousness as a means of community development/social transformation as opposed to the Washingtonian model of economic self-empowerment without a change in status.

Although Du Bois is considered by many to be the father of black studies, his contemporaries, B. T. Washington and Marcus Garvey, played an important role in the creation of a certain ethos among blacks that gave way to the creation of community development/social transformation. Washington set the stage for white philanthropists who were liberal and had a desire to play a role in designing the new black community. Garvey is credited for the Ethiopic sentiment among blacks in the diaspora. He felt that if diasporic blacks could work together with blacks in the continent of Africa, then neither would remain the victims of white oppression. The ethos created by the ideas of these two great men gave way to the understanding that blacks would no longer be defined by their past of slavery, as a new negro had arisen from the pit of servitude.

This new ethos brought about an era that would later be called the Harlem Renaissance. In the 1920s, blacks began to move into the area of New York known as Harlem and other cities of the north and midwest such as Chicago. Many of these newcomers to the Harlem area were poets, artists, and writers. This talented group of individuals took as their subject matter the essence of blackness. The literature and other forms of culture developed during this period placed emphasis on expressing a true black worldview in its entire variegated splendor as opposed to what blacks had become as a result of racism. While studying at the Sorbonne, a Martinician named Aimé Césaire met a Senegalese student named Léopold Senghor. Together they studied classics of Western culture. Apart from these studies, they came across the writings of Alain Locke and Du Bois concerning the new era of self-definition for blacks. The writings of these architects of the Harlem Renaissance pushed Césaire and Senghor to the concept of Negritude. Negritude became the precursor to the slogan of the 1960s and 1970s that "black is beautiful."

Each man returned home and continued to write poetry and other philosophical works. Senghor involved himself in politics while Césaire became an educator and activist. One of his most notable students was Frantz Fanon. Fanon wrote four books, two of which influenced Malcolm

X. These writings along with the writings of Marcus Garvey and also the teachings of Elijah Muhammad influenced Malcolm X to develop his own concept of raising consciousness.[20] Malcolm X's charismatic speeches encouraged blacks in general and specifically those of the black power movement to take part in what is typically known as black consciousness.[21] Martin Luther King was also an influence on this movement, but the leadership or vanguard for this movement did not develop among the usual hegemonic structures within the church.[22] Those who were a part of the vanguard for this movement consciously decided that they would act on the traditional structures of society, rather than be acted on by them. They created a vision and an ideology of community separate from the white mainstream thought,[23] one that challenged others who had not been as active in creating a vision that was separate from white ideology.

Huey Newton contributed to this ideological shift first by being one of the founding members of the Afro-American Association from which developed the movement for Black Studies departments in American colleges and universities. Second, it was the intent of the Black Panther Party, under Newton's direction, to not only influence the consciousness of blacks through a new political theory (as opposed to the rhetoric of prominent black leaders of his day) but also encourage a generation of blacks, who lived out the philosophy of black humanity espoused by Malcolm X. The ideas in Howard Thurman's *Jesus and the Disinherited*, written in 1949, can be identified in the writings and sermons of African American theologians.[24] It is to be noted that the most prominent of these theologians, James Cone, is also credited as being the father of black theology.

SCOPE OF THE STUDY

This research uses primary sources from the works of both Howard W. Thurman and Huey P. Newton. Most of the works published on Howard Thurman have been synoptic in format and have attempted to give a detailed coverage of his works. For this reason, the author felt compelled to focus only on those works of Thurman that are necessary for a complete account and understanding of his idea of consciousness as a freestanding concept, the development of this idea, and its usage as the fundamental premise from which his ideology was shaped.

Huey P. Newton was different from Thurman in that Newton spent most of his time engaged in political activism. Therefore, Newton's works, with the exception of his dissertation and autobiography, took the form of position statements and political essays. As Newton's collective writings are not as extensive as Thurman's, his entire corpus of four books and also several political essays, which are not included in the published works, are used as primary sources. However, the process of analysis for Newton's works will be the same as for Thurman's works. The works will be dissected to find an idea of consciousness as a freestanding concept, the development of this idea, and its usage as the fundamental premise from which his ideology was shaped.

CONCEPTUAL FRAMEWORK

To develop a clearer understanding of the connection between experience and the modalities used by each writer to accomplish his respective goal, it was necessary to approach this study through a critical method rooted in an Afrocentric paradigm. This paradigm also aided in gaining a better understanding of the desired goal of each writer. Primary data sources were employed except where it became necessary to show how the writers' works were perceived by others. In these instances, secondary sources were used to demonstrate consistency and points of contrast between the author's views and those from prior research. Qualitative analysis is the research design employed in this study, using Afrocentric methods of interpretation concentrating on an African aesthetic to extract the purpose and means through which consciousness was used in the writings of the research subjects. The method used bears a close resemblance to the phenomenological method of Heidegger, except that the focus will also be on the individual's connection to a community, culture, and the phenomenon being studied. Content analysis gave this author the ability to determine how the idea of consciousness migrated and developed through the writings of each subject, specifically in reference to the development of the definition of consciousness and its usage as a conceptual base from which to develop the author's own ideas of community development/social transformation.

In summary, this book analyzes the writings of two men of African descent through the lens of the African diasporic experience with special attention given toward defining this type of ontological experience from an Afrocentric perspective. "Afrocentricity is essentially a quality of perspective or approach rooted in the cultural image and human interests of African people."[25] In effect, Afrocentricity gives the researcher the ability to interpret the thoughts and actions of people of African descent as a normative event in accordance with the lived experience of the people. This means that the ideas, thoughts, or actions that arise in this moment cannot be thought of as eccentric, obscene, or abnormal behavior, but instead are thought of as the standard. In other words, Africans can stand center stage acting in their own history, instead of being acted on by history.

Afrocentricity as an academic concept was developed by and is based on the writings of Molefe Asante, who wrote a defining text in 1980 titled *Afrocentricity: The Theory of Social Change*. In this work, Asante purports that Afrocentricity is a philosophical perspective associated with the discovery, location, and actualizing of African agency within the context of history and culture.[26] Accordingly, Afrocentricity equips the theorist and practitioner with the ability to perform proper analytical interpretation with regard to the African experience. The central tenet of Afrocentricity is Njia. Njia is the collective expression of the Afrocentric worldview based on the historical experience of African people. Njia demands a divestment of alien views and values so that the individual is transformed by African principles and values.[27]

Once this transformation occurs, research performed from this perspective must transition from black studies to Afrology. Afrology or Africology is a pan-African system of analysis that centers on Africa when focusing on the aesthetic, political, and geographic dimensions of the African collective will. This concept essentially is an outgrowth of an African worldview. Ghanaian philosopher Kwame Gyekye puts forth the idea that an African worldview is possible because threads of an underlying affinity run through the beliefs, customs, value systems, and sociopolitical institutions and practices of various African societies. Gyekye goes on to argue that the African worldview is a component of African culture and also functions as a unifying interpretive reference point for African peoples, and therefore also functions as a common philosophical component of the discipline of Africana Studies, giving it a common philosophical framework.

In essence, what Gyekye and other Afrocentric scholars such as Vernon Dixon are suggesting is that studying the experiences of blacks using Eurocentric methodologies leads to different intellectual trajectories than the same study would yield using an Afrocentric methodology.

In fact, a fundamental basis for all Africana studies has been agreed on by most Africana Scholars as consisting of three major components: subject matter, perspective, and goal. From these key components, it is thought to necessarily follow that Africana studies can be defined as a critical analysis of the Africana experience, people, and culture, through the usage of the African worldview, with the ultimate goal of changing the life of African-descended people.

These components, and specifically the Africological methodology they support, are products of culture as are others' worldviews and methodologies. According to Vernon Dixon, the research methodology one chooses by his or her axiological or value orientation influences directly "the content and therefore the models or hypotheses."[28] From culture, understandings of the good, bad, beauty (pleasure), the grotesque, and ultimately what is divine are embedded in the deep recesses of human intellect. Culture can be said to create certain appetites and aversions. This understanding of culture is extremely important because of the role that culture plays in determining perception, both individual and communal. Perception is the single determinant in how an experience will be interpreted. Kariamu Welsh-Asante devotes much attention to perception as a derivative of culture. She defines aesthetics as "the science of perception," which supports the idea of using an aesthetic lens to analyze others' thoughts as conveyed in their writings.[29]

Inasmuch as aesthetics is defined by Kariamu Welsh-Asante[30] as a science of perception, this definition is tantamount to this research which analyzes the writings that two individuals used to describe certain phenomena. However, maintaining consistency with an African worldview requires the implementation of an aesthetic that is Afrocentric. Fortunately, much attention in the modern era was given to creating a description of an aesthetic that arises from the culture of Africans in the diaspora. The first major attempt to describe this aesthetic during the modern era was made in Alain Locke's compilation, *The New Negro*. This attempt was an ambitious struggle to describe the meaning of blackness through the historical and creative writings of talented people concerned with, as the title suggests, divesting themselves of the descriptive proclamations that were born of slavery.

According to Locke, blacks were seeking to change the image of their relationship with whites. This effort was necessary because the nature of the relationship was already changed but many false images remained. Blacks were still looked at as objects having no contribution to their own experience or others. Locke wrote, "The Negro now becomes a conscious contributor and lays aside the status of a beneficiary and ward for that of collaborator and participant in American Civilization."[31] In other words, blacks were conscious, had creative impulses, and should be treated on par with other Americans.

The next extensive explication of the African aesthetic took form in the writings of the creators of Negro culture, specifically Aimé Césaire. Césaire was a part of an intellectual circle that included Léopold Senghor, Leon Damase, and others. They produced a passionate tract against assimilating in which he coined the term "Negritude." Césaire believed that his African ancestry could be found at the core of his being and he wanted to create a theory that would encompass his new reality. Negritude, as described by Césaire, was a decoloniza-tion of consciousness as well as a struggle against assimilation and alienation. It was an intentional attempt to show that Africans were not barbarians but indeed human beings with the determination to create and interpret their own reality-based experience. Negritude's primary aim was to present a profile of the African personality.

Stephen Henderson compared Negritude with the African American concept of soul, which he described as emphasizing intuition, dance, the power of words, wholeness, and harmony. However, Amiri Baraka's work is considered the single most important connective link between Negritude and the period in African American literature known as the black arts movement from which developed the black aesthetic. In *Black Fire*, co-authored with Larry Neal, a new black aesthetic is presented over and against the aesthetic presented previously by Alain Locke. Those who participated in this aesthetic were conscious of the obstacles created by the political structure as well as those created by the cultural memory of the formal institution of slavery. This aesthetic was not permanent, but served as a transitory bridge that led to the development of Afrocentricity and the aesthetic which ensued.

Afrocentricity developed because the worldview of black Americans was disrupted by a half century of struggling against Eurocentric thought. Afrocentricity is a mode of thought and action in which centrality of African interest, values, and perspectives predominate.[32] Two major pro-ponents, and possibly founders of Afrocentricity, are Maulana Karenga and Molefe Asante. Karenga and Asante were concerned mostly with methods being implemented in the study of Africans and diaspora. Karenga focused on the historicity of the histories being told. Karenga's assumption was that Eurocentric philosophers such as Hegel, Kant, and the like created historical philosophies that the Western world would use to create a frame of reference to interpret the past, giving rise to an understanding or consciousness of what it means to be. Asante focused his concerns on the subject–object relationship between blacks and whites. The issue of black people's active participation in the creation of the history in which they were a part was central to Asante's concerns. Through the perspective of the Eurocentric philosophers, it was thought that blacks were a passive part of history. This way of thinking was damaging because it caused blacks to be unconscious of the activity propagated by their ancestors in the determination of their own reality. Both Asante and Karenga saw their ideologies as transformative agents that had the ability to reform the way blacks understood themselves. In fact, Asante referred to Afrocentricity as a metatheory, a theory or grounding point from which to build other theories. This metatheory accordingly grew out of the lived experience of the African people, whether in the diaspora or on the continent.

Whereas this type of meta-theoretical thought developed within the departments of African and African American Studies (AAAS), there have been many, particularly in the departments of philosophy where AAAS has its roots, that have volleyed criticisms at the premises of this type of thought. One criticism stems from the foundational claim of the proponents of Afrocentricity that Afrocentricity conceptually is developed from African thought and culture. These critics question whether there is a direct enough linkage between African thought and those in the diaspora such that the development of an Afrocentric thought could develop outside of Africa and still be considered African. This debate has its roots in the ideological sparring of E. Franklin Frazier and Melville Herskovitz. It was these sparring sessions that brought to the forefront the misrepresentation concerning effects of slavery outside of the African diaspora and whether or not this effect has caused a significant perceptual change from African to Western blacks. There is currently an ongoing debate concerning claims to African culture in the diaspora. Afrocentric scholars continue to insist that "Africanness" is innate and the only reason it does not have a more profound appearance is because diasporic Africans have been taught to suppress their culture in order that they might defer to Western culture.

In addition, Afrocentric scholars are criticized for the usage of the label Africology to describe the methodological approach of studying all Africans (including the diaspora). This is because the term is developed through the reason of a Greek system of nomenclature. The problem in the usage of this terminology to describe the study of Africans is that the name Africology carries certain assumptions of how the suffix "-logy" is derived from the Greek work logos, which represents the unifying principle of Greek philosophy. Greek usage of logos assumed the oneness of all knowledge. This becomes problematic because it then necessarily follows that regardless of the starting point, Afrocentric and European scholars should reach the same logical conclusions. This line of reasoning means that if these conclusions are not reached, then the study is tainted. Scholars such as Lewis Gordon suggest that the concept of Djed found in Egyptian mythology is more suitable than logos. Djed refers to the four pillars representing stability as portrayed in the ancient Kemetic/Egyptian mythic life. The backbone of Osiris is the symbol used to represent Djed, and its usage has to do with creating stable, permanent, and durable knowledge. Although Djed is represented by a spine in many writings, it is equally represented by a tree. The major separating conception that Djed would add to an Afrocentric theoretical framework is that implicit in the meaning of Djed is transformation. This is significant in that it is in keeping with a major proclaimed goal of any Afrocentric research effort.[33]

Finally, the focus on classical African society (Egypt) has created a type of conundrum for those arguing that the classical past is the goal for any type of community development/social transformation. This creates a tension for those whose only link to Africa exists in cultural memory. Educationally, the organizational infrastructure does not exist to propagate such a cultural exchange on a scale that large. Admittedly, a return to African classic civilization has appeal to some; however, Egypt was not a utopian society. Diaspora blacks who go to the African continent looking for a grand welcome have been a little put off by stares and shouts of "obrunie," which is a Ghanaian word for whites. The disconnect is greater than many imagine. There also exists the push by younger Africans to be less African by adopting many of the cultural trappings of the West. Many times, this westernization is tied to income. Used Western clothes are sold at incredibly cheap prices compared with traditional African clothing. Afrocentricity does little to address non-Afrocentric thinking on the continent.

CHAPTER ORGANIZATION

The introduction has presented the background and main focus of this study. It also presented a summary of relevant writings that contribute to the conversation concerning consciousness as a subject matter during the modern era of African American studies. The foundational material on which this study is based and the methods which it follows are also brought to the fore. In the second chapter, a deeper review of the relevant literature takes place with a twofold purpose: first, to locate this study within the context of the general discussion about consciousness, and second, to demonstrate the participation of African American writers in this conversation. The context and historical overview of the aesthetic tradition that supports this study is also given attention, focusing on how this tradition connects many African American writers such as the two who form the fulcrum of this study. In chapters 3 and 4, the knowledge-shaping experiences of Howard Thurman and Huey Newton are outlined to investigate the source of their ideas of consciousness. In chapter 5, their ideas of consciousness are examined in detail to determine the nature of the confluence that exists in their writings and to explicate how their ideas of consciousness drove their understanding of community development and social transformation.

NOTES

1 The modern era is defined here as the period from 1896 (conferring of PhD to W. E. B. Du Bois) to 1975 (the end of the Vietnam War).

2 Gayraud S. Wilmore, *Black Religion and Black Radicalism: An Interpretation of the Religious History of African Americans* (Maryknoll, NY: Orbis Books, 1998), 100.

3 Huey Newton's book, *In Search of Common Ground*, was not published until 1973; however, the discussions from which the book was written took place in 1971. The book was copyrighted and published in 1973. Howard Thurman's book, *The Search for Common Ground*, was copyrighted in 1971 and published in 1973.

4 Howard Thurman, *The Search for Common Ground: An Inquiry into the Basis of Man's Experience of Community* (New York: Harper & Row, 1971), 89–104.

5 Wade W. Nobles, *Seeking the Sakhu: Foundational Writings for an African Psychology* (Chicago: Third World Press, 2006), 81.

6 Luther E. Smith, *Howard Thurman: The Mystic as Prophet* (Washington, D.C.: University Press of America, 1981), 1.

7 Walter E. Fluker, *They Looked for a City: A Comparative Analysis of the Ideal of Community in the Thought of Howard Thurman and Martin Luther King, Jr.* (Lanham: University Press of America, 1989), 7.

8 Carlyle Fielding Stewart, "A Comparative Analysis of Theological-Ontology and Ethical Method in the Theologies of James H. Cone and Howard Thurman" (PhD diss., Northwestern University, 1982), Proquest Dissertations and Theses (8226025), 1–2.

9 Mozella G. Mitchell, *Spiritual Dynamics of Howard Thurman's Theology* (Bristol, IN: Wyndham Hall Press, 1985), 1.

10 Ivory L. Lyons, *The Idea of Sin in the Work of Reinhold Niebuhr and Howard Thurman: A Confluence toward Justice* (Claremont Graduate University, 1998). Proquest Dissertations and Theses (304447019), 1.

11 James H. Cone, *Black Theology and Black Power* (New York, 1969), 5.

12 Wilmore, *Black Religion and Black Radicalism*, 235.

13 Leonard E. Barrett, *Soul-Force: African Heritage in Afro-American Religion* (New York: Anchor Press, 1974), 4–7.

14 Mark Anthony. Neal, *Soul Babies: Black Popular Culture and the Post-soul Aesthetic* (New York: Routledge, 2002), 3.

15 John T. McCartney, *Black Power Ideologies: An Essay in African-American Political Thought* (Philadelphia: Temple University Press, 1992), 139–45.

16 Erik H. Erikson and Huey P. Newton, *In Search of Common Ground: Conversations with Erik H. Erikson and Huey P. Newton* (New York: Norton, 1973), 9–12.

17 Bobby Seale, *Seize the Time: The Story of the Black Panther Party and Huey P. Newton* (New York: Random House, 1970), 66–68.

18 Kariamu Welsh-Asante, *The African Aesthetic: Keeper of the Traditions* (Westport: Greenwood Press, 1993), 63–73.

19 Ibid., 19.

20 James H. Cone, *Martin & Malcolm & America: A Dream or a Nightmare* (Maryknoll, NY: Orbis Books, 1991), 52–57.

21 Seale, *Seize the Time*, 82.

22 Huey P. Newton, *Revolutionary Suicide* (New York: Harcourt Brace Jovanovich, 1973), 163–70.

23 Ibid.

24 Howard Thurman, *Jesus and the Disinherited* (New York: Abingdon-Cokesbury Press, 1949), 49–50.

25 Nathaniel Norment, *The African American Studies Reader* (Durham: Carolina Academic Press, 2001), 361.

26 Molefe K. Asante, *Afrocentricity: The Theory of Social Change* (Chicago: African American Images, 2003), 3.

27 Norment, *African American Studies Reader*, 361.

28 Karenja K. Carroll, "Africana Studies and Research Methodology: Revisiting the Centrality of the Afrikan Worldview," *The Journal of Pan African Studies* 2, no. 2 (March 2008): 4–8.

29 Welsh-Asante, *African Aesthetic*, 1.

30 Ibid.

31 Alain LeRoy Locke, *The New Negro* (New York: Simon & Schuster, 1997), 8.

32 Asante, *Theory of Social Change*, 2.

33 Lewis R. Gordon, *An Introduction to Africana Philosophy* (Cambridge: Cambridge University Press, 2008), 109.

REVIEW OF LITERATURE

African diaspora culture was originally forged into a common unit, containing some superficial variations, during the unbearable pressure created by the movement of Africans through the Middle Passage. It is for this reason that many of the same inspirations and concepts can be found in the writings of thinkers who used diverse means in order to create their oeuvre, particularly during the modern era of African American studies. There is a confluence of thought that exists among African American thinkers that stems from a particular connection to and participation in a deep cultural memory.

In this chapter, the way will be paved for a more sustained development of the arguments put forth in the previous chapter by outlining the central tenets of each man's idea of consciousness, their usage of the idea of consciousness as the foundation of community development/ social transformation, and those philosophical concepts that connect Newton's ideas to those of Thurman. This literature review begins with a brief review of those works about Thurman and Newton included in this study. Next, in order to facilitate an understanding of consciousness as the driving force of community transformation, an investigation into the historical nature of the understanding and arguments concerning communal consciousness has been appropriated. Literature of a philosophical nature expounding on African American culture is then utilized to explain the theory of the social aesthetic. Following this will be a discussion of the use of *Kugusa Mtima*[1] from a strengths perspective as the general theoretical framework for this study. This will be done by first creating a foundation for the discussion of aesthetics as a field of philosophical inquiry. Then, in order to formulate an explanation for the existence of confluence in the writings of these thinkers, especially one that hinges on a cultural link between writers of the African American modern era, selected writings from this period in the categories of philosophy, politics, religion, and literature will be investigated.

HOWARD THURMAN

According to Dr. Luther Smith, "Thurman was a mystic who recognized the necessity of social activism for enabling and responding to religious experience."[2] It was religious experience, according to Smith, that was the aim of life. Smith's book, *The Mystic as Prophet*, critically examines the connection between experience and the individual's relationship with The Holy in the writings of Thurman.[3] As a companion to that work, Smith also compiled the work *Howard Thurman: Essential Writings*.[4] Another useful collection by Walter Fluker and Catherine Tumber, *A Strange Freedom*, seeks to present Thurman's works in a topic-oriented fashion with a brief commentary on each work based on the situations that served as the impetus for the writings themselves. Mozella Mitchell's examination of Thurman's writings and thoughts is also important to this study because of the attempt to identify the central concept(s) on which Thurman's work was created. She accomplishes this task by examining seven of Thurman's works in light of the theological and literary horizon in which they were produced.

HUEY NEWTON

Erik Erikson referred to Newton as a radical theorist in his collaborative work (with Newton, *The Search for Common Ground*). Judson Jeffries used this characterization as the title for his work analyzing Newton's political theory. Judson critically examines Newton's writings using the theories of prominent political theorists to demonstrate the value and depth of thought in the work of Huey Newton. *Seize the Time* by Bobby Seale connects the life of Newton to the developmental history of the Black Panther Party. As cofounder of the Black Panther Party, Seale shares unique insights into the manner in which the experience of Newton served as the major driving force for the creation of a specific type of organization with a specific ideology. The edited collection of Newton's works was compiled by David Hilliard and Donald Weiss and is titled *The Huey P. Newton Reader.* In this work, the editors sought to create a timeline of Newton's thoughts by including portions of Newton's works according to the time period they were created. This anthology is important also because it contains some works that heretofore were unpublished. Hilliard is also the author of an informative biographical work, *Huey: The Spirit of the Panther,* which details names, places, and situations that formed the consciousness of the Panther movement. Several important essays concerning the critical examination of Newton's ideas were included in *The Black Panther Party Reconsidered* by Charles E. Jones. Although apologetically written, it is important because many of the writers also had firsthand knowledge of the effect that the ideas of Huey P. Newton had on his milieu.

THE STUDY OF CONSCIOUSNESS

Consciousness, and the nature thereof, has been a much studied phenomenon in the discipline of philosophy. It is not until the modern period that Rene Descartes attempts to use his inquisitive form of reasoning to get at the nature of consciousness that has contributed to most of the discussion that is today centered on the study of mind and its correlation to consciousness. Descartes struggled to use pure reasoning to determine what the essence of Being is. In this quest, he used a methodology of doubt to determine that the essence of Being was mind.[5] Notwithstanding the problems created by his mind–body dualism, it is agreed that Descartes did establish that the individual is conscious and is conscious of being conscious.

After Descartes, Thomas Hobbes attempted to put forth a theory of collective consciousness based on the metaphysical understanding of individual consciousness. Hobbes was insistent that the universe consisted of only matter in motion.[6] He was convinced that anything that did exist was material and that there was no such thing as a nonmaterial thinking substance that could cause movement. Movement, even in humans, was a direct result of a mechanical network of causes. Hobbes also used his metaphysical understanding of the universe as the foundational explanation for his political theory. He first dissolves civic and personal bonds into the atomic, original condition, the state of nature. Then, he shows how to use these minimal materials to rebuild a state that, according to Hobbes, will really work. It seems that he was also successful in creating a theory of collective unconsciousness in that these particles were to be confined in a field so-called the state. Following this combining, these particles will act in some predictable manner not determined by the individual particle, but determined by the collective whole.

Around 1900, the movement of phenomenology arose under the guidance of Edmund Husserl, which sought to give new vitality to philosophy by stressing the need to turn to the pre-scientific phenomena of ordinary life and to describe them without reliance on scientific assumptions. This suspension of scientific thought allowed a new openness to problems and traditions considered dead or irrelevant, and after the First World War, it inspired many remarkable inquiries in theology, ethics, political philosophy, aesthetics, and classical philology. But perhaps most striking and unexpected was its contribution to metaphysics in Martin Heidegger's renewal of the question of Being.[7] This combined, in a startling fashion, a deeply probing recovery of Greek philosophical texts with a radically anti-academic account of the human existential situation that was shaped by Heidegger's reading of Kierkegaard and Nietzsche, and by the mood of crisis following the disastrous world war. Heidegger understood Being as the hidden and elusive ground of all that is speakable and thinkable.

DEFINITION OF AESTHETICS

In order to study consciousness, we must study its effect. This is done by observing patterns of behavior to determine clues from which to analyze and define subjective experience. Once this subjective experience is defined, it can then be categorized. A major category of subjective experience is that of aesthetics. Many cultural appendages develop and are valued because of a particular aesthetic. Some examples of this phenomenon are types of religious expression, uses of language in speech and literature, and also the social and political arrangement of a society. For the purpose of this study, the history of this framework from about the eighteenth century from African, African American, and European cultural traditions will be examined. The existence of this framework brings to the surface certain analytical issues or queries, the first of which stems from the necessity to know "What exactly is art?" Art, according to Immanuel Kant,[8] is a perceptible form that has the ability to stimulate the senses by eliciting thought concerning the object's ability to evoke thought without consideration being given to any concepts separate of the perceptible form. In other words, art exerts pressure on the observer by provoking a strong conscious response not based solely on what the observer sees in the form. Benedetto Croce, a twentieth-century philosopher, put forth the concept that art is the expression of emotion.[9] Leo Tolstoy went further, asserting that art was the communication of emotion from one person to another through indirect means.[10] Mimesis, imitation, or representation is also taken to be art by modern thinkers such as Langer, Goodman, Danto, and Walton.[11] Danto advances this discussion further by expressing the need for art to fit or find meaning within a specific cultural framework or social institution identified by its constituent rules and roles.

Next to be examined is how the methodology that is used to perceive and critique aesthetic properties should be chosen. It stands to reason that the perception of the perceptibility of many properties may be culturally specific. For example, according to Zora Neale Hurston, an aesthetic property found in the black artistic use of language is the double descriptive (i.e., the boy fell down; the man was killed dead, etc.).[12] In European culture, this is not considered an aesthetic property; it is considered redundant. Many in the past have considered the process of choosing a methodology, and the methodology itself, to be universal. This universalizing has led to many works of art going unnoticed or having faced undue harsh criticism. The universalizing of the methodological process has also misrepresented the historical worldview and tastes of the African diaspora. Many have considered diasporic aesthetic preferences to be merely black imitations of their European counterparts. Therefore, it is crucial to any study of the aesthetics to know the process and the framework used to choose the methodology before blindly accepting a particular interpretation of a work of art.

Economy of space prevents the listing of all methods created from the 1800s until the present in their entirety. For this reason, only major examples will be explored. The three major areas of philosophy, which some would probably term original areas, are epistemology, ethics, and ontology/metaphysical.[13] From the three areas of philosophy listed, epistemology—which is a study of how humans know—is the area from which aesthetics is derived. This connection to epistemology has created a natural association between methods chosen for epistemological studies and the methods used for aesthetic studies. Aesthetics also went through several phases. The first use of the word *aesthetics* and a systematic approach to aesthetics took place in 1735.[14] Alexander Gottlieb Baumgarten introduced the term in his dissertation titled "Philosophical Meditations on Some Matters Pertaining to Poetry." Aesthetics, in the words of Baumgarten, is defined as "the science for directing the inferior faculty (as emotions are considered to be inferior) of cognition or the science of how something is to be sensitively cognized."[15] The Earl of Shaftesbury, Joseph Addison, Jean-Baptiste Dubos, and Francis Hutcheson actually used the term previously but did not define it in a systematic way.[16] However, the term did not become interchangeable with the philosophy of art until the posthumous publication of Georg Wilhelm Friedrich Hegel's lectures on aesthetics.[17] Hegel, along with Kant and Schiller, formed the groundwork for what is considered the development of Western aesthetics.

John Dewey's social aesthetic philosophy is critical to this research; however, before moving forward to discuss the aesthetic system of John Dewey, it is necessary to speak for a moment about the aesthetic methodology of Karl Marx simply because his system of aesthetic critique initiated a dramatic shift in aesthetic criticism by acknowledging that the universality found in the Kantian critique, of which Hegel was also a major proponent, was demolished. Marx's materialistic system of thought is built on the idea that the only reality is a physical reality.[18] Marx agrees with other scholars of his day that human understanding of the world arises from consciousness; however, Marx describes his understanding of the development of the human consciousness by saying that life is not developed by consciousness, but that the consciousness is developed by life. This simply means that material conditions can change the way humans think. Marx's approach is usually referred to among scholars as dialectical materialism. His theory rests on the tenet that all of human history can be traced through the struggles between classes. He drew from history, philosophy, and economics in order to understand the true causes of class contradictions and conflicts. Western scholars consider how Marx's theory applies to aesthetic oppression because of the connection culture has to history, philosophy, and economics.

With this brief explication of the Marxist approach to aesthetics, a transition can now be made to the aesthetics of John Dewey. John Dewey's work is pivotal for this study because of his emphasis on the tension between what is called the aesthetic experience and the lived experience, creating the groundwork necessary to justify portraying Thurman and Newton as social aesthetes. Much of Deweyan philosophic thought in general, and particularly his thought concerning the aesthetic, "suggests that associations can assist individuals in perceiving the relationships between themselves and the contemporary fragmented social environment and encourage them to creatively use this information to inform their political action and political selves."[19] Dewey goes further to say that the appetite for a particular type of society and for the pleasure derived from living in the same society is deeply affected by the connection the individual feels to the other individuals or institutions in that society. It is significant to understand Dewey's thought to perceive that he reaches back to the eighteenth century to dispute Kant's concept of the separation between fine art and natural beauty. Dewey applies his concept of aesthetics in a broader construct to include all aspects of society.[20]

John Dewey argues for a connection between fine art and all creative processes, inclusive of the beauty found in nature. This connection between aesthetic analysis and all creative processes is not new to aesthetic thought. Kant, in the *Critique of Judgment*, acknowledges that aesthetic analysis can be applied to all aesthetic experience inclusive of the beauty found in nature.[21] Schiller also followed this line of logic and admits to owing a great debt to the thought of Kant. Schiller applies his understanding of aesthetic analysis to the aesthetic experience of being a part of a political state and having a vision of the ideal state. Accordingly, he proffered that it becomes necessary to continue to work until the actual political state and the ideal state are one or at least close enough to create the desired aesthetic experience for the individual. Although Hegel believed that there should not be any connection between fine art and the aesthetic experience offered by nature when it comes to the study of aesthetics, he does offer points for consideration in the examination of the work of Dewey. The concepts of spirituality and freedom are seen throughout the writings of Hegel but are only applied to the fine arts. Dewey borrows these concepts; however, in contrast to Hegel, he applies them across the full spectrum of aesthetic experience, not just the fine arts that are intentionally created with an aesthetic aim of evoking the aesthetic moment.[22]

Dewey focuses much of his philosophical thought on what he refers to as "the lived experience."[23] The attention he gives to this type of aesthetic experience places him in the category of a social aesthete. This description is accurate because of Dewey's engagement and preoccupation with the ability of individuals to self-actualize based on how they are affected through their lived experience. Basically, individuals, according to Dewey, develop appetites or aversions depending on the amount of pleasure derived from being a member or nonmember of a particular community. Much of the cause of the affection is contingent on the arrangement of the particular community/society. He defines "the lived experience" as entities interacting in certain ways.[24] Dewey further purported that an experience must have continuity, that an experience produces knowledge, and that certain types of experiences produce specific types of knowledge. Aesthetes are affected by these experiences at higher levels and interpret them in various ways to give them direction in order that others may take notice of them and become more conscious of their effect.

The connection that Dewey makes between all experiences and the aesthetic creates space for an aesthetical critique of politically constructed society. In *Art as Experience*, Dewey writes, "In an experience, things and events belonging to the world, physical and social, are transformed through the human context they enter, while the live creature is changed and developed through its intercourse with things previously external to it."[25] Dewey claims that it is associations that cultivate needed individual characteristics such as trust, communication skills, political confidence, tolerance, and other characteristics needed by the modern democracy. Accordingly, Dewey felt that the modern society in the United States in particular, with its emphasis on individualism, deceived and greatly hindered the individual's opportunity to fully participate in democracy.[26] He blamed this condition on the fact that individuals had a fragmented experience in U.S. society, causing a lack of knowledge concerning political power and discouraging political action. Accordingly, social aesthetics and the actions of the social aesthete become critical in enabling communities to actualize their full political freedom.

THE AFRICAN AESTHETIC—*KUGUSA MTIMA*

This book makes use of the African aesthetic, specifically the concept of *Kugusa Mtima* developed by Mirimba Ani, as the interpretive framework for comparing the idea of consciousness in the writings of Thurman and Newton, focusing on their usage of consciousness to develop their theories of community development/social transformation. The intent is to explain the perceived appearance of confluence in their writings. *Kugusa Mtima* means "to touch the heart" as defined by Mirimba Ani using Kiswahili.[27] The concept was created as an attempt to explicate the term *aesthetic* from an Afrocentric perspective. African aesthetic as a philosophic phenomenon and an academic area of concern can trace its roots to the beginning of the modern period of African American studies; however, it was not until the age of Afrocentricity that diasporic scholars initiated the usage of African concepts and linguistic devices to assist in the explication of this concept. To be sure, there is a black aesthetic tradition that was initiated during the Harlem Renaissance but matured during the Black Arts Movement. It was created using a reactionary methodology that was based in the same philosophic traditions as that of the Eurocentric aesthetic models, which gave little latitude to address the Africanness of diasporic black cultures.

Kugusa Mtima gives nomenclature to the idea of an Afrocentric aesthetic conceived with the intent of being a corrective to the Eurocentric critical analyses of the African diasporic experience. Spirituality and collective behavior are considered to be the essence of the phenomenal experience of being African. This essence has had little variation in the diaspora. These concepts are foundational to the design of the *Kugusa Mtima* framework. Ani reaches back to the African society and transposes these phenomenal experiences forward to create a paradigm that expands the concepts of beauty/pleasure, which are synonyms for aesthetic experience, to include transcendence, transformation, human consciousness, and the power of a collective human will. The conceptual aim is to include an African worldview in the interpretation of diasporic experience.

Ani accomplishes her aim through the creation of an aesthetic conceptual framework that is born of African ideals and is linguistically of African descent, strategically using Kiswahili terms to describe particular aspects of the African diasporic culture that can be evidenced as proof of an African aesthetic. This technique was pioneered by Alexis Kagame in response to the work edited by Placide Tempels in 1945.[28] Tempels, a young Belgian missionary, produced "Bantu Philosophy," which called into question certain philosophies, such as those of Hegel and Hume, that defined the African continent as having no worldview. Excited by this work, Kagame changed his focus toward explicating Bantu philosophy from a Bantu perspective. In his critique of Tempels, Kagame was careful to insist on the existence of a universal African ontology. He took inspiration from writers, such as Léopold Senghor and Aimé Césaire, who created the concept of Negritude based, in part, on the Harlem Renaissance and on the idea of the solidarity of the black world.[29] Many writers (such as John Mbiti and Robert Farris Thomas) followed Kagame, specifically using African terms to express African concepts.[30] Ironically, one of the most notable writers to perform this task is a German writer, Janheinz Jahn. Jahn's book, *Muntu*, attempts to make the concepts found in writings of Kagame and other continental Africans more accessible to those who were to study them in the West.[31]

All of these writers had their own perspective of what an African-derived descriptive philosophy entails; however, it appears that each was attempting to make known the phenomenon of the African world-view being overlooked as a legitimate school of philosophical thought so as to defraud the world of its existence. The same has been the case with descriptive philosophies and the analysis of the cultural memory embedded in the African diaspora. In many ways, these philosophies have been created to act as a corrective to the Eurocentric philosophies. They also had the intent of creating an ontology of blackness, according to Victor Anderson.[32] Examples of this ontology appear in the writings of many; however, this analysis will be confined to those writers who specifically mention the effect of aesthetic experience on black social consciousness.

In *Discourse on Colonialism*, Aimé Césaire describes the creation of the concept referred to as Negritude. Césaire describes Negritude as a philosophical critique of black Antilleans who identified with French ideologies, assimilating these cultural ideas into their writings. According to Césaire, the writing of Antilleans became colorless, having totally rejected their own culture in favor of an alien school of thought. He describes Negritude as an attempt to dis-alienate from the colonization of culture by the French. Although Césaire agreed with

Karl Marx, he felt that Marx's approach did not go far enough in terms of answering the question of racial oppression. Césaire felt that emancipation consisted of more than political emancipation. A significant connection he shared with the subjects of this study was the influence of the Harlem Renaissance on this movement, of which he said, "I felt that the movement in the United States created an atmosphere that was indispensable for a very clear coming to consciousness."[33]

Blues People was an attempt to describe the "cultural gene" that developed from LeRoi Jones's desire to trace the origin of an African American culture that could be said to be over and above African culture.[34] To this culture, Jones gave the name that was already a part of the vernacular—"Negro," which was offered to the world by the Europeans but given understanding and shape through the actions and experience of the New World African. Jones describes this culture by writing, "the reaction and subsequent relation of the Negro's experience in this country in his English is one beginning of the Negro's conscious appearance on the American scene."[35] In this work, it is Jones's intent to intimate exactly how the experience of the African American created the blues and jazz through its ability to portray the consciousness of the people at the moment, to speak to that consciousness, and to also lift that consciousness, much the same as a religious myth becomes a part of the moral fiber of a community or nation. Jones's description of this phenomenon also gives insight into the African diaspora's culture through its birthing of what might be called an African American cultural genetic code.

Leonard Barrett's *Soul-Force* was a monumental attempt to describe in vivid detail the essential qualities of the inward nature of black life that has given blacks the ability to survive the horrors that have accompanied their experiences in a foreign land.[36] According to Barrett, "It was [the black man's] quality of 'soul' that finally leavened the bread of calculated materialism, and his suffering finally evoked guilt in the conscience of his oppressors which brought sanity and humanity to New World."[37] This work created the framework for the discussion of a cognitive awareness that grew from the depth of the black experience. Barrett's nomenclature for this cognitive awareness was not original, and was already being used in the black vernacular. "Soul" or "soul-force" was the instigator of black culture. Barrett proves this by analyzing black humanistic expression.

Barrett's book is important and unique because it is a work that for the first time attempts to encapsulate this awakening of consciousness into a specific period of time. He uses the beginning of the Garveyite Movement as the beginning of this period of awakening. For Barrett, it was at this juncture that blacks began to recreate their identity. This ideology allowed the masses of blacks to participate in a communal movement they could understand because it arose from the common experience of being black. In this new consciousness, the seeds for a black aesthetic were also contained. According to Barrett, the conscious understanding of blackness gave blacks the ability to reinterpret the past, understand the present, and plan the future. Barrett's work is also unique because it considers all the movements from Garvey to the Black Power Movement as one movement. This point of view makes space for this writer's concept of the freedom movement. For Barrett, the development of soulforce created a pleasurable experience resulting in a mass movement, not just for blacks in America but also the world over.[38]

The idea of analyzing the experience of black people and artistic works created by writers of African descent using a culturally based aesthetic began in earnest during the early 1900s with W. E. B. Du Bois and the writers of the Harlem Renaissance.[39] It was during this time period that the conceptual framework for the black aesthetic and its logical conclusion were conceived. Then, just as now, there were proponents and critics. In a 1926 article titled "Criteria for Negro Art," W. E. B. Du Bois argued that black writers had a responsibility to transform reality through their writings: "Thus all Art is propaganda and ever must be." He went on to say that he was unashamed to write black writings to gain the right for blacks to "love and enjoy." However, Du Bois's idea of transformation for black writers was that they should become equal to white writers in the acclaim they received. It was not his goal to identify the characteristics that made black writing unique.

Not all writers of the Harlem Renaissance thought as Du Bois. Langston Hughes, in his 1926 article titled "The Negro Artist and the Racial Mountain," put forth the idea that black writers should write from their experience.[40] He did not want the black writer who wrote from the black experience to feel inferior. He wrote in response to those who felt that to write from black experience cheapened the literary product. Hughes believed that black culture was valuable and did not need to mimic white culture. Similarly, Zora Neale Hurston created an argument to support this conception in her 1934 essay, "Characteristics of Negro Expression." She argued that blacks had developed not only a culture but also an aesthetic through which the culture was experienced and interpreted.[41] She believed that there was an interpretation of English that was unique to blacks and went even further to create a list of some of the characteristics of black speech and writing patterns. Richard Wright, in a 1937 essay titled "Blueprint for Negro Writing," also expressed a similar view to that of Hurston. This shared view was that as a theme in black writing, these characteristics sprang forth through the black writer's personal encounter and manipulation of the experience of black people, a-historically, as if the total cultural experience that is blackness happened in one generation.[42] This activity of remembering, retooling, and reusing the experience of blackness as a sort of cultural genetic unit, according to Wright, has the ability to "lift the level of consciousness" of black writers.

Although many disagreements existed concerning the exact purpose and strategies of diasporic artistic creations, few, if any, critics as well as artists would disagree that a basic cultural memory could be identified in these creations stemming from a common aesthetic experience and common cultural memory. These two elements in concert have strongly contributed to the confluence that exists among artists and major thinkers of this period. This confluence, according to Afrocentric thinkers, developed as a direct result of being forced to accept blackness and give up tribal or ethnic connections as a result of the great M'AAFA, or transatlantic slave trade. This aesthetic moment was simultaneously buried deep within the soul of the black slave memories of being a Fulani, a Wolof, an Akan, a Fante, and so on, and gave rise to the African, which was represented fully in the black diaspora, thus also giving rise to the freedom aspect of the African aesthetic.[43]

Finally, it is also necessary to state that there was a philosophy of freedom that was developed during slavery, but it was not canonized until the 1800s with the academic writings of W. E. B. Du Bois.[44] Its aim was community development/social transformation, which it considered to be dependent on having a national consciousness rather than economics. The Africans who were enslaved in the Americas had an image and conception of themselves that was derived from their cosmology and image of God; however, this image was redefined to match the existential conditions in which they found themselves.

NOTES

1 Welsh-Asante, *African Aesthetic*, 65–66 (see chap. 1, n. 18).
2 Smith, *Mystic as Prophet*, 45–48 (see chap. 1, n. 6).
3 Ibid.
4 Howard Thurman, Walter E. Fluker, and Catherine Tumber, *A Strange Freedom: The Best of Howard Thurman on Religious Experience and Public Life* (Boston: Beacon Press, 1998), 1–18.
5 René Descartes, *Meditations* (New York: Liberal Arts Press, 1951), 127.
6 Thomas Hobbes, *Human Nature and De Corpore Politico* (New York: Oxford, 1999), 51.
7 Martin Heidegger, *Being and Time* (Albany: State University of New York Press, 1996), 114.
8 Albert Hofstadter and Richard Francis Kuhns, *Philosophies of Art and Beauty: Selected Readings in Aesthetics from Plato to Heidegger* (Chicago: University of Chicago Press, 1976), 277–89.
9 Jerrold Levinson, *The Oxford Handbook of Aesthetics* (Oxford: Oxford University Press, 2003), 5–16.
10 Ibid.
11 Ibid.
12 Winston Napier, *African American Literary Theory: A Reader* (New York: New York University Press, 2000), 31–44.
13 Hofstadter and Kuhns, *Philosophies of Art and Beauty*, 277–89.
14 Jerrold Levinson, *The Oxford Handbook of Aesthetics* (Oxford: Oxford University Press, 2003), 5–16.
15 Ibid.
16 Ibid.
17 Hofstadter and Kuhns, *Philosophies of Art and Beauty*, 277–89.
18 Karl Marx, *Selected Writings in Sociology & Social Philosophy* (New York: McGraw-Hill, 1964), 269–70.
19 Jason Kosnoski, "John Dewey's Social Aesthetics," *Polity* 37 (2005): 193–215, accessed April 20, 2012, http://www.palgrave-journals.com/polity/journal/v37/n2/abs/2300009a.html.
20 Jerrold Levinson, *The Oxford Handbook of Aesthetics* (Oxford: Oxford University Press, 2003), 104.
21 Immanuel Kant, Nicholas Walker, and James Creed Meredith, *Critique of Judgment* (Oxford: Oxford University Press, 2007), 157–59.
22 John Dewey and John J. McDermott, *The Philosophy of John Dewey: Vol. 1, The Structure of Experience. Vol. 2, The Lived Experience*, two Volumes in One (Chicago [u.a.]: Univ. of Chicago Press, 1981), 253.
23 Ibid.
24 Ibid., xxv.
25 John Dewey, *Art as Experience* (New York: Putnam, 1958), 257.
26 Welsh-Asante, *African Aesthetic*, 62–79 (see chap. 1, n. 18).

27 Ibid.
28 "African Philosophy More," African Philosophy (Bruce Janz), accessed February 25, 2015, https://pegasus.cc.ucf.edu/~janzb/papers/37AfPhil.pdf..
29 Aimé Césaire, *Discourse on Colonialism* (New York: Monthly Review Press, 1972), appendix.
30 *African Philosophy and Religion* by John S. Mbiti and *Flash of the Spirit* by Robert Farris Thomas fill in the lacunae created by Kagame through the explanation of the African Cultural Worldview.
31 Janheinz Jahn, *Muntu: An Outlinse of the New African Culture* (New York: Grove Press, 1961), 99–100.
32 Victor Anderson, *Beyond Ontological Blackness: An Essay on African American Religious and Cultural Criticism* (New York: Continuum, 1995), 132.
33 Césaire, *Discourse on Colonialism*, 26–27.
34 Amiri Baraka, *Blues People* (Edinburgh: Payback Press, 1995), ix.
35 Ibid.
36 Barrett, *Soul-Force*, 9–10 (see chap. 1, n. 13).
37 Ibid.
38 Ibid.
39 Locke, *New Negro*, 2–4 (see chap. 1, n. 31).
40 Napier, *African American Literary Theory*, 103.
41 Ibid.
42 Ibid.
43 Robert Farris Thompson, *Flash of the Spirit: African and Afro-American Art and Philosophy* (New York: Random House, 1983), 7–11.
44 Du Bois was the first scholar of African descent to produce scholarship describing the experience of the diaspora.

3

THURMAN'S KNOWLEDGE-SHAPING EXPERIENCES

INTRODUCTION

There must be always remaining in every man's life some place for the singing of angels

—Thurman[1]

It is possible to study a theologian in several ways, depending on the interest one has in the theologian concerned. One might be purely interested in the theology, the starting points, the concepts used, the main arguments, and the conclusions as a result of all this. One could explore the historical, social, and cultural context in which this theological work takes place, what it is influenced by, or which elements of its context it has its influence on. One may want to get to know the person behind the work and try to understand a theological style and content by studying the theologian's education and encounters in life or even try to unravel the theologian's personal character itself.

Theologians are usually involved in a variety of contacts and communities. They are usually not and should not be mere academics. Nor are they or should they work entirely in service of the church. Especially in the twentieth century, when they played an important role in a rapidly changing culture, theologians were involved in different contexts. Apart from working in the church, continuing its search for self-understanding and self-expression, theologians have been teachers and researchers at universities and schools, journalists, and politicians; they have been involved in cultural debates on ethical matters, the arts, and inter-religious communication. But most of them have been working in a local context, dealing with pastoral, personal, and communal matters.

Theologians usually operate in several of the aforementioned contexts at the same time. Biographies of theologians therefore usually require the description of a theological life on several levels concurrently: theological, socio-cultural, and personal. The story of the theologian's life is most compelling for someone interested in people who lived and worked at the center of a certain socio-cultural context in a certain age. Such is the case with Howard Thurman. Howard Washington Thurman's birth was at a moment in time when much of the world concentrated on the physical being of a human and gave little thought to the inner spiritual being. The African American existence in the South was still centered on agricultural production. Although higher education was a possibility for African Americans, it was still a distant dream for most. Thurman was born in Daytona, Florida, on November 18, 1899, four years after the Plessy versus Ferguson decision, which adjudicated "separate but equal" to be legally acceptable treatment of blacks in the United States. This decision, along with the memory of slavery, helped to shape the childhood memories of the young Thurman. Uniqueness of experience is not found in Thurman's phenomenological account of his life. What is unique is the way the experience is appropriated throughout his complete intellectual life.

THE SOCIAL MYSTIC

Thurman's efforts toward social change, as described by Alton Pollard, have been little noted. Of the many reasons that are most plausible, timing and method are foremost. In the context of timing, Howard Thurman seems to be a prophet sent to a people out of due season. He was too young to be a part of the Niagara movement and the founding of the National Association for the Advancement of Colored People (NAACP). When the great race riots of the early 1900s took place, Thurman was entering college. By the time Martin Luther King led the Montgomery Bus Boycott, Thurman was in his mid-fifties. Thurman was sixty-three during the March on Washington, and 66 by the founding of the Black Panther Party. Although Thurman's life seems unsynchronized with major events in the freedom movement, this is probably not the predominant reason for the historical slight Thurman has received from scholars. His methods for addressing the social problems of the day were probably the most prominent reason for the Thurman void in history.

Mysticism as a way of life and knowing the Ultimate has been applied frequently to the person of Howard Thurman; in fact, several of Thurman's writings focus on the subject and some even use the term in the title. In defining the term, Thurman relies on the definition given by Rufus Jones, a Quaker mystic: "The word mysticism is used to express the type of religion which puts the emphasis on the immediate awareness of relationship with God, on direct and intimate consciousness of the Divine Presence."[2] This definition, for Thurman, was congruent with his personal perception of his spiritual relationship with God, and much of Thurman's intellectual energy was given to interpreting the experiences he accepted as contact with the Ultimate. One such experience is found in the many meditations in front of the big oak tree located behind his boyhood home. Thurman writes in his biography, "As for me, on each visit I would go to my oak tree to lean against it for an intense moment of past intimacy."[3]

There are profound implications for Thurman's understanding of his brand of mysticism to be found in his conception of community. For Thurman, community was the pinnacle of human "beingness," and the best of what it means to be human is found in human community. Thurman considered the opposite of community to be isolation. Of isolation, Thurman writes, "The human spirit cannot abide the enforced loneliness of isolation."[4] He also writes, "We literally feed on each other; where this nourishment is not available, the human spirit and the human body both sicken and die."[5] Several events happen during the period of isolation that force on the mystic a strong desire for community. The act of introspection specifically occurs during this period of isolation. Thurman writes that the unique characteristic of introspective thought is that it creates solitariness in the midst of others because it cannot be truly shared with others. Despite the solitariness of life, Thurman understood the nature of life to be social in expression. He purports that life is expanded into its fullest creative potential by life's experience. The social aspect of this experience is that life's unity actualizes this potential. Therefore, for Thurman, isolation severely limits potential. However, the solitariness of the individual's experience also creates the possibility for the aesthetic vision through the unity with God. So then, according to Thurman, community is realized potential and its germ is a basic characteristic of life itself. In other words, the desire for community is drawn from the individual, which of necessity is already present, and is simply realized through the experience of being alone or isolated.

On the contrary, Thurman interprets the definition of mysticism given by Jones as the "response of the individual to a personal encounter with God within his own spirit."[6] This definition and the actions of most who are considered to be mystics obfuscate the very definition of a social mystic. Historically, those who have been considered to be mystics have led lives filled with such asceticism that a great part of their being has been characterized as alienation. Mystics have focused on creating a relationship with the Ultimate. Anything that lessened this relationship with the Ultimate was usually relegated as insignificant as far as life is concerned. This involves fasting, abstinence from sex, and isolation in terms of social relations. These characteristics along with others caused Jones to divide mystics into two diverse types of consciousness, namely negation mystics and affirmation mystics.

Negation mystics act from the perspective that the experience of God or God's attributes cannot be found in fullest potential in our world. Our world contains only material or physical objects. These physical objects are mere finite appearances, but God is infinite in nature; therefore, God is otherworldly. When negation mystics contemplate, the existential condition of their surrounding environment, they become dismayed and realize that the only way to recreate the aesthetic experience of the mystical creative encounter with the Holy is to remove themselves from the possibility of becoming fixated on the finite so as to focus on the infinite. For the negation mystic, this requires a life filled with focus on God, absent from the glare of that which has the ability to block the vision of the Holy.

Affirmation mystics, on the contrary, do not make the vision the end of life, but rather, the vision and the accompanying aesthetic experience are the beginning. Like the negation mystics, they desire to have the immediate, firsthand experience with God, but not just for the pleasure of the experience. Instead of seeking the absolute through negation, affirmation mystics find the revelation of God in the existential or lived experience. Rather than avoid the finite, they seek God in the finite. Affirmation mystics see the realization of the vision in the advancing of God's kingdom. They have beheld a glimpse of the aesthetic vision created by the Holy and are forever conscripted to join the Creator in making their desired experience their lived experience. Thurman's writings convey his familiarity with the theological understanding of affirmation mystics, and he clearly uses this understanding in his faith and practices. He uses a quote from Eugene Deiss to epitomize his understanding of the connection between his lived social experience and the fulfillment of the vision received from God. Thurman writes, "while there is a lower class, I am it. While there is a criminal element, I am of it. While there is a man in jail, I am not free."[7] Thurman believed he had to also deal with social injustice as well as personal injustice, so that the vision of the Holy would remain free from obstructions emanating either source of injustice.

The period of isolation is also the moment when the individual realizes a need for spiritual discipline through the reception of the aesthetic vision from God:

> In the total religious experience we learn how to wait; we learn how to ready the mind and the spirit. It is in the waiting, brooding, lingering, tarrying timeless moments that the essence of the religious experience becomes fruitful. It is here that I learn to listen and to swing wide the very doors of my being, to clean out the corners and crevices of my life so that when His presence invades, I am free to enjoy His coming to Himself in me.[8]

Thurman describes the benefits of spiritual discipline through this statement. For Thurman, the discipline does not bring about the vision or encounter, but it does create space to allow for clear reception of the vision. The mystic's strong desire for a primary community with God creates a need to perform practices that would create this space. It is in isolation, mental or physical, that the mystic's aesthetic experience, or as Thurman refers to it, the creative encounter derived from the vision, becomes the desired experience. This contrast between the desired experience and the lived experience is what gives purpose to the discipline of the spirit.

In Christianity, there is ever the central, inescapable demand of surrender. The assumption is that this is well within the power of the individual. If the power is lacking, every effort must be put forth to find what is hindering it. Thurman begins this act of surrendering by analyzing the self to determine those attributes that are prohibitive to

God or to God's essence returning or to being remembered within the human body. However, he then realizes that the individual cannot be removed from his lived experience. If one is to attain oneness with God, the lived experience must be conducive to this process. In line with this process, he believed that any mental idea or bodily feeling that hindered surrender was vestigial in nature and the individual was better off without it. As this practice relates to the greater human community, an ethical stance must be taken by the mystic if the desired experience and the lived experience are to become one. In *The Mystic as Prophet*, Smith writes, "Thurman's primary identity was that of a mystic, a mystic who recognized the necessity of social activism for enabling and responding to religious experience."[9] Thurman calls this brand of mysticism the social mysticism.

The social mystic, or mystic activist as referred to by Alton Pollard, believes that because of the creative encounter, personal transformation and social transformation are both necessary to actualize the desired experience. This is in large part due to the concept that social mystics, including Thurman, have of sin. Sin becomes anything that causes difficulty in beholding the vision. Thurman writes, "He comes upon the fact that deep within his own personality and life are the things which obscure and blot out vision."[10] In other words, the struggle with impulses, with inner division, unworthy desires, and purely self-regarding tactics, including the whole world of egocentric manifestations, are all regarded as an indispensable part of the defect of his vision. The mystic's desire is to have the experience or encounter with the Holy as often as possible; however, the mystic soon grows into an understanding that personal thoughts and their actualized manifestations affect this aesthetic experience of being in the presence of the Holy.

The mystic soon realizes that it is not just the personal conceptions and their actualization that hinder the desired experience, but also that their counterparts in other individuals cloud the perception of the vision for the whole of humanity. For Thurman, the mystic determines the ethics of an act by whether it leads to the mount of vision or away from the mount of vision. In other words, what is supposed to "be" is tied to the vision. Anything less than the vision is unacceptable for the mystic. To this end, the social mystic, according to Thurman, must constantly work toward the achievement of the vision. Thurman believed that the ultimate goal of human life is to know God, who created a unity and equilibrium in the individual and has the ability to do the same in a community. Accordingly, for Thurman, whatever was possible in the community meant the same would be possible throughout the world.

Thurman writes, "The social mystic sees that the world of things and men does not conform to the unity which he has experienced in his vision."[11] The implication in this passage is that Thurman and others holding a similar aesthetic aim derived from a developed aversion to their lived experience find it impossible to not facilitate change. Thurman never spoke in terms of the impossibility of removing obstacles that obscured the vision of God. In fact, his version of social mysticism held that the thesis of life is God or oneness with God. The antithesis is man separated from God or unconscious of the oneness that exists in the universe. Mystic experience then becomes the synthesis of the desired spiritual equilibrium. After having experienced this mystic unity, Thurman was unable to live without working toward the goal of involving as many people in the experience of the vision.

EXPERIENCE

Experience for Thurman was paramount and should be intentionally and constantly reflected on, in the interest of remolding and retooling the lived experience so that it eventually reflects the desired experience. According to Dr Luther Smith, Thurman repeatedly asks, "How can I believe that life has meaning if I do not believe that my own life has meaning?"[12] For Thurman, the lived experience and the knowledge gained from that experience shape the individual's consciousness. This in turn gives the individual, in this case Thurman, the ability to interpret his or her connection to the world. Essentially, the theological witness is used by him to answer the eternal questions of life and living. These answers gave him the ability to increase consciousness and create unity within the community of which he was a part. He felt that these answers were not available to the non-reflective thinker for the reason that the intentional performative act of thought demonstrates the desire to transform the lived experience into the desired experience. Therefore, without reflection, no answer can be found because the non-reflective thinker does not desire to find an answer.

For Thurman, the reflections on his early life served as a rudder guiding his course on the sea of experience. Much of his early reflection centered on his situation in life, which was mainly that of being a young black male growing up in a segregated black community: "The fact that the first twenty-five years of my life were spent in Florida and Georgia has left deep scars in my spirit and has rendered me terribly sensitive to the churning abyss separating white from black."[13] For Thurman, it was his lived experience that gave the impetus to seek out the truth of life that superseded his present condition, so that he could achieve his desired experience. The death of Thurman's father, Saul Thurman, was one such early reflection that left deep scars in his spirit. In fact, for Thurman, this moment was the catalyst for his acute sense of awareness that while the church was necessary for a certain type of communal experience, the individual's experience and communion with the All began in solitude.

DEATH OF FATHER

According to Thurman, his father was a powerful man, gifted both physically and endowed with inner fortitude. Thurman reports that he never saw him sick until he contracted pneumonia in 1907. It would be this disease that would cause the demise of Saul Thurman. Saul's death was a moment and an experience that would prove to be an awakening moment in the consciousness of Thurman. The moment of crisis came when Thurman's father was denied funeral service because he was not a member of any church. Eventually, the church relented at the insistence of Thurman's grandmother and allowed the funeral to take place, but it was not with the blessing of the pastor. Indeed, the pastor refused to eulogize Thurman's father, and he had to be eulogized by a traveling evangelist, Sam Cromarte, who gave a eulogy that the young Thurman never forgot. As Thurman would later describe the eulogy, it was as if his father was being preached into Hell.

The description Thurman provides for the atmosphere surrounding his father's death and the ensuing change in his life demonstrates the level of reflection that he would perform for years to come and would become his signifying quality. He writes in his autobiography, at the age of seventy-nine, "death was well known in our community."[14] It is difficult to infer from this statement that this was the sentiment of a seven-year old boy. It is more plausible that this statement was developed through years of contemplation focused on creating an understanding of him, and the experiences which were to become a filter through which he would subjectively interpret his life and the experience of being black. There begin to appear implications for Thurman's strong desire to be in a community. Although he initially met this desire with denial and rejection, it was a formative moment that would be the catalyst for Thurman's conclusion that it is a sin to do anything that would hinder or destroy the community. He implies in his biography that the church had sinned through its refusal to grant Saul Thurman a proper funeral. This event was an antecedent to his desire to know the nature of the life-causing agent within us and its connection to God, a desire that would shape the cause of his future studies.

RUFUS JONES/HAVERFORD

It was at Haverford that Thurman was allowed to study mysticism in full measure for the first time; however, it also allowed him to realize that he did not want to do doctoral studies. It would be difficult to quantify exactly the effect of Thurman's studies with Rufus Jones. It is possible, however, to determine whether there was a qualitative change on Thurman's writings based on ideological statements, vocabulary changes, and references directly to Jones's and Thurman's statements before and after. For instance, Thurman's first complete statement concerning mysticism came in 1939 when he published a set of lectures that he delivered a year earlier at Eden Theological Seminary. "Social Mysticism" was the title of the lecture series in which Thurman details the point at which he joined the mysticism discussion. Thurman wrote sparingly concerning his studies at Haverford, and it seems as if he needed time to allow his studies to become a part of him. The only way to extensively analyze the effect this experiential moment had on his consciousness is to critically examine his description of mysticism in this first complete statement of his mystic ideology.

According to Walter Fluker, Thurman's most prominent concern was the ethical responsibility of the mystic.[15] Thurman places mysticism squarely in the center of the discussion by first addressing the common belief that mystics desire to only lead solitary pious lives. This point is disputed in the statement that the life of the mystic is worked out in the world of men and things. According to Thurman, the oneness of life creates a feeling of aloneness; thus, although the mystic experiences the power of intimacy with the All, the aloneness also creates a desire to be in community.[16] This communion with others must take place in time and space. For this reason, the ethics of life—how does the temporality of life affect how we live?—become a major consideration for the mystic. The desired experience for the mystic is to know God with the whole self. Mystics have a heightened perception of the presence of God, which creates a desire to feel the pleasure constantly. This creates tension between the lived experience and the desired experience. In the lived experience, there exist moments that frustrate the sensation of the All for the mystic. The mystic also comes to realize that even if he is exalted through the disciplines of the spirit, there still remain those other struggles caused by conflicts between individuals, communities, and cultures that cannot be ignored.

In this set of lectures, Thurman also treated the idea of consciousness for the first time. Consciousness is divided into two categories: self-consciousness and communal or social consciousness. In both cases, consciousness is defined "as acting reflectively upon experience."[17] The individual or group takes notice of inner and outer phenomena, given the ability to respond appropriately, which means some type of communication must take place in order for the moment to be shared. According to Thurman, the struggle for selfhood is included in the mystic experience of aloneness and the desire for unity. The mystic desires this unity with the All in God. The mystic experience also allows the mystic to have a vision of life's possibilities, clearly recognizing the rhythm that is present in the unity created through the connection of God and the individual.

Thurman began to now incorporate the ideas gained through the experience of Haverford. It is evident when comparing this lecture series with his earlier writings that his general understanding of experience, especially as it concerns God, was expanded ontologically through language and also through the use of this new language to explain his lived experience. For example, he describes all life as one, and also places much value on the mental activity involved in accessing the benefits of the mystic experience.

In a 1927 essay titled "Finding God," Thurman describes the unity of God and of human experience; however, what is curiously absent is the idea that there are some who have a greater connection or at least propensity to take advantage of such a connection by virtue of their strong desire to seek a more intense experience with the holy. In this particular essay, Thurman defended this premise based on the ability of all humans to have the same levels of experience and makes no exception for the mystic. He writes,

> First of all, if God is the source of all life, if out from Him emanates all creation, then there must be an underlying unity for all then and whenever one digs in honestly, living up to the limit of all that one has at the particular time, one does make contact with that unity.[18]

After the Haverford experiential moment, Thurman also argued the idea of a separate mystic experience available only to those who seek it with great desire. Accordingly, Thurman writes,

> In his act of worship the mystic achieves a transcending unity. His self-centeredness is resolved in a higher synthesis. God possesses him . . . The meaning of life for him is summarized in the vision of the good, which he [the mystic] has thoroughly experienced. The vision makes mandatory that he be good so as to stand ever in immediate candidacy for the reception of God.[19]

The vision creates its own need for reconciliation with the lived experience. It allows the mystic to arrive at the realization that the lived experience is full of dissonance and lacks the rhythm necessary to experience God for any duration. However, it is the mystic's desired experience to develop consonance such that the physical world is brought into rhythm with the spiritual.

Finally, before Haverford, Thurman appears more concerned with the practice of being a Christian as opposed to the experience of being with God, and having covered a multiplicity of topics, his writings were not focused. According to Dr Fluker, "Jones provided Thurman with a critical methodology to explore his belief that one could devote oneself to the ultimate concerns of the human spirit without neglecting the pressing moral issues of society."[20] The manner in which these points are best demonstrated is twofold. First, much of Thurman's religious writings are aimed at reconciling his experience of being black with being Christian. This conflict altered his perception and he seemed convinced that black ministers should dedicate energy to the transformation of black people through teaching personal responsibility and communal responsibility. He soon transitioned from this thought pattern to a more inclusive gospel relevant to all people. He continues to use Jesus as the ultimate example of how community should project itself into the world; however, he does not yet seem to explore the transformational possibilities that exist in the teaching of the mystic consciousness. While at Haverford, he studied the mystics and came to grips with mystical experience. Among the mystics studied were Meister Eckhart and many other Spanish mystics. Although Thurman's residence at Haverford lasted only five months, this experiential moment affected his personal study and also affected his very being. Thurman's later writing demonstrates this point. After Haverford, he began to use the language of mysticism to explicate the phenomenon of being in the presence of God and the transformation that it causes.

GANDHI

Thurman visited Gandhi in 1936, making him the first African American to do so. Several African Americans such as B. E. Mays and Mordecai Wyatt Johnson would follow this pattern; however, for Thurman, this experience not only served as confirmation that the spirit and experience of the Divine were universal but also forced him to reconcile the conflicting relationship between African Americans and the Christian faith as practiced in the Western society. Thurman believed that the Western church had betrayed Christianity through its allowance and justification of social inequalities. Thurman wrote in *Jesus and the Disinherited*,

> The desperate opposition to Christianity rests in the fact that it seems in the last analysis to be a betrayal of the Negro into the hands of his enemies by focusing his attention upon heaven, forgiveness, love, and the like.[21]

In this statement, Thurman deals squarely with the subject matter of the book. "Negroes," according to Thurman, have their backs against the wall by virtue of the oppression they have experienced. Thurman seems to imply that ignoring social injustice and then teaching love is inconsistent. Jesus taught love; however, his teachings also challenged social sins.

The Gandhian experience challenged Thurman's thoughts and in many ways buttressed his faith. First, Thurman saw that the idea of nonviolence could be a useful tool especially for blacks in their struggle for relief of oppression. He quotes Gandhi in his autobiography as saying "that with a clear perception it could be through the Afro-American that the unadulterated message of nonviolence would be delivered to all men everywhere."[22] Thurman did not inquire about Gandhi's impetus for the statement; however, it can be assumed that it was said because of the exposure African Americans received during the struggle for freedom. This statement continued to challenge Thurman's religious thought even during the writing of *Jesus and the Disinherited*. It is portrayed in Thurman's focus on the suffering that Jesus experienced so that others might recognize their unethical behavior. This is the concept of redemptive suffering that was utilized by Thurman again in *Disciplines of the Spirit*, in which he discusses the necessity of people who are willing to suffer so that the world may survive. Thurman was already a pacifist, convinced to be so by his grandmother after being involved in a fight during grade school, but he had not yet considered nonviolence a powerful force until the Gandhian experience.

Second, Thurman was determined to reconcile his own theological beliefs with the obvious conflicts of racism and Western Christianity. After arriving in Ceylon, Thurman was confronted by a gentleman when he had finished giving lectures. The man questioned Thurman about his presumed betrayal of his race and other darker people of the world by taking a journey to represent Christianity. Thurman was perceived in this manner because of the history of Christian involvement with slavery and oppression throughout the world. On his return from his voyage, he wrote a two-part reflection of his trip titled "What we may learn from India," in which he deals with the historical reasons for Christianity's relationship with racism and oppression. In this work, he also examines the difference between American racism and racism in India. This paper remains incomplete, but the thought is carried over to *Jesus and the Disinherited*. Thurman is convinced that confessed Christians are able to be racist and also tolerate racism because of their connection to Jesus as an object of worship instead of as a subject.

Finally, Thurman would coordinate all of his theological thoughts and actions by balancing them on personal experience with God and what he would come to call the religion of Jesus. As has been indicated previously, much of Thurman's writing was focused not on a superficial profession of Christian faith but on a much more introspective level by reflectively focusing on what he believed to be the true religion of Jesus. This can be seen in the subject matter—from how to discipline the spirit, to dealing with an encounter with the Holy creativity, to finally creating common ground with all humanity. However, Thurman was also interested in causing the fellowship he shared across racial and religious lines in India to manifest itself in the United States, a nation that professed to be Christian. He would accomplish this grand task by resigning his post at Howard and co-founding the Fellowship Church for All Peoples.

KNOWLEDGE

Thurman's experience, both as a mystic and being black in a segregated America, created a specific type of stored information subjectively filtered through the perceptive processes that informed his individual consciousness. It also shaped his understanding of social consciousness as it related to community development and social transformation. The verbal display of this information is evident in many of his written works. For the purpose of this study, only those works that are necessary for a complete understanding of Thurman's idea of consciousness as a freestanding concept, the development of this idea, and its usage as the fundamental premise that shaped his ideology will be discussed. In order that these concepts may be explicated fully, certain queries must be made into the relevance of the work and the part the specific work plays in explaining Thurman's idea and usage of the concept of consciousness.

Because Thurman was not a systematic theologian or philosopher, his writings are not arranged in any particular order except as to make a complete historical and experiential whole. The goal for Thurman is to explain how the desire to create an experience that could not be hindered by life's conflicts overwhelmed the whole of his life and was the impetus to his writings. This overwhelming motivation drove Thurman to search for clarity within his life, and this point is also made clear through the fact that his writings show direction and intentionality toward the goal of creating this reality.

The first of these writings to be examined is *Deep River and the Negro Spiritual Speaks of Life and Death*. This work is unique in the fact that initially it was published as two separate writings in two different years of the 1940s, but because of the similar nature of the content, they have now been published as one work.[23] In this work, Thurman explains that in the Negro spirituals, it is evident that these songs were used to inspire the African slaves to continue to press forward toward freedom while continuing to endure the horror of their immediate circumstances. Thurman also purports that the spirituals provide inspiration for their posterity to endure and overcome bitter circumstances. The book centers around the subject matter in the words of the spirituals and their usage as the groundwork for a philosophical worldview. That worldview can be stated simply: the African slaves were a people who refused to allow their desired experience to become diminished by their lived experience. The spirituals served this purpose by becoming a convenient canon of culture easily transmittable from one slave to another concurrently while going through the drudgery of life.

Thurman demonstrates this process from the beginning of the book by explaining the role of the Negro preacher as proponent, teacher, and perpetuator of this philosophy. The Negro preacher is described as the greatest single factor in determining the spiritual destiny of the slave community.[24] According to Thurman, the Negro preacher accomplished this by creating a framework from which to build hope on both individually and communally. Despite the restrictions placed on them, these preachers were moved by the belief that all humans were God's children, and taught that God would bring about the end of suffering in this life. The Negro preacher could identify with the plight of the slaves because the preacher recognized that their total environment was created for the purpose of shaping their minds and spirits by the premise of their utter worthlessness, which was only lifted by the load given to them through the slave master. Thurman writes, "there is a bottomless resourcefulness in man that ultimately enables him to transform 'the spear of frustration into a shaft of light.'"[25] Accordingly, when this message of being children of God was preached to the preacher's fellow slaves, it began its work in shaping a new way of perceiving themselves in relation to their surroundings. This new cultural aesthetic gave birth to the religious folk songs now known as Negro spirituals.

Thurman shows that through these spirituals, the belief in God's ability and willingness to deliver all his children from evil can be witnessed. This is shown through the selected verses used by Thurman to demonstrate the new perception of the slaves. One such song has the following lyrics: "When Israel was in Egypt's land, Let my people go, Oppressed so hard they could not stand, Let my people go." In this song, there is identification with the children of Israel's bondage. Slaves did not see themselves as singing about a phenomenon that was to occur but once. They believed firmly that any of the children of God experiencing oppression would receive deliverance at the hand of God. When describing the slave's understanding of God, Thurman writes, "God was the deliverer. The conception is that inasmuch as God is no respecter of persons, what he did for one race [God] would surely do for another."[26] Also, inherent in this statement is the premise that God is able to meet the evil situation head on and achieve victory. In the spirituals, there is no doubt of the ability of God based on the history and testimony of God's people.

The spirituals also served to unify the slaves' thoughts and desires, creating a nation within a nation. Unofficially, the spirituals formed a very important part of the religious education. This was done by merging the spirituals with the scriptures through their lived experience. To do this, the slave used the inspiration of both the Old and New Testaments of the Bible. The aesthetic that was formed through their experience was used to inform them of which scriptures applied to their lived experience. Thurman writes of this,

> When I was a boy it was my responsibility to read to my grandmother, who had been a slave. She would never permit me to read the letters of Paul, except on occasion, the 13th chapter of First Corinthians. When I was older, this fact interested me profoundly. When at length I asked her the reason, she told me that during the days of slavery, the [white] minister on the plantation was preaching from the Pauline letters—Slaves, be obedient to masters to your masters, etc. I vowed to myself, she said, that if freedom ever came and I learned to read, I would never read from that part of the Bible![27]

Second, not only did they use their experience and aesthetic to choose passages, but they also used these tools to change the very scripture itself. For example, according to Thurman, instead of posing the question that was posed by Jeremiah, slaves chose to use the affirmative and state "There is a balm in Gilead."[28] This statement was possible because of the optimism that was embedded in the culture premised on scripture and cultural memory. There is also the prevailing concept that the slave could and possibly would have to transcend this reality to be free. However, the desire for freedom was not just confined to this world. Thurman puts forth the idea that the slave was constantly faced with the imminent threat of death.

The next work to be analyzed is *Jesus and Disinherited*.[29] This work was written during a period in Thurman's career when he was serving as the minister of the Fellowship Church in San Francisco. In the preface of the book, Thurman insisted that the book's major purpose is to deal with the issue of the significance of the religion of Jesus to those with their backs against the wall. When Thurman was touring India, he was asked by Gandhi if he had not in fact betrayed his people by becoming a Christian. Thurman's answer to Gandhi, which becomes the subject matter of *Jesus and the Disinherited*, and the Gandhian experiential moment in time led him to realize that this question had not been well answered by Christian theologians. In fact, in the first chapter, Thurman recounted the reasoning behind the writing of the book, which accordingly arises from the paucity of sermons he had heard on the subject of what the religion of Jesus does for those whose backs are against the wall. This is what Thurman focused on during the remainder of the book.

Thurman's use of the phrase "the religion of Jesus"[30] seems to separate him from the institutional church and also describes an approach to an ontological concept of the religion denoted by the name Christianity. It was clear to Thurman that the historical connection of Jesus to slavery and other human atrocities lessened the image of what was then itemized as the Christian religion. Thurman recounts this historical connection in part by the acts of the so-called Christians in support of the slave trade. The failure of theologians of his day to respond to this history created a conundrum for many people who were culturally, economically, and physically affected by such actions. This is why Thurman was considered to be a traitor to the darker peoples of the world by serving as a representative of the Christian church during his trip to India, Ceylon, and Burma, which was also sponsored by the Young

Men's Christian Association (YMCA).[31] In many ways, *Jesus and the Disinherited* serves as an intellectual attempt by Thurman to put to rest any misrepresentations of his ideological stance on the connection of Jesus to the institutional concept of the church and the racism which was allowed to thrive within the institution. Thurman has recently come under criticism for putting a utopian emphasis on the Christian faith. Any reference to him by scholars that attempts to criticize his belief in the ability of humans to create what appears to be a utopian society by focusing on the Holy, and eradicating those things that hindered this focus, has the appearance of being less than genuine and does not take into account Thurman's analysis of the subject/object relationship of Jesus.

Thurman accomplishes his goal by underscoring Jesus's relationship to humanity through the development of the frame of reference from which the teachings of Jesus arose. This was done to show that the teachings of Jesus took on a particular form because of the form of life from which they arose. In other words, Jesus saw and interpreted the world in which he lived from the perspective of a small-town, poor, Jewish male, responding to a world that was ordered to the advantage of those whose lives were representative of the essence of power that was a consequence of their nationality, wealth, and ethnicity. Thurman is clear, however, that Jesus was not the only Jew found in his predicament, but he was emphatic that living in such conditions at a time when the Jewish national existence was very precarious would have had a profound effect on the individualization of Jesus. For Thurman, this is evidenced by many of the teachings Jesus espouses concerning Jewish attitudes and actions when in the presence of Roman citizens and soldiers. For example, "And whosoever shall compel thee to go a mile, go with him twain."[32] In this scripture, as in others found in this text, Thurman interpreted Jesus's teachings by pointing out that Jesus realized the ineffectiveness of attempting to change the mind of the oppressor without first giving a reason for the change. According to Thurman, this is done through the changing of the psychology or consciousness of the Jewish nation with which to engage in redemptive suffering. He likens the teachings of Jesus to a survival program for an oppressed people. This is explained by the fact that it is religion born in the mind of a teacher of Jewish descent suffering extreme oppression:

> The core of the analysis of Jesus is that man is a child of God, the God
> of life that sustains all of nature and guarantees all the intricacies
> of the life process itself. Jesus suggests that it is quite unreasonable
> to assume that God, whose creative activity is expressed even in
> such details as the hairs of a man's head, would exclude from his
> concern the life, the vital spirit, of the man himself.[33]

This statement is indicative of the premise Thurman uses for the remainder of the work. He was convinced that Jesus's religious mission was completed by teaching the oppressed Jewish nation a new consciousness, which was to view themselves through a lens that was not shaded by the Roman perception, but one that was based on what he called the "awareness of being a child of God."[34] Thurman was adamant that Jesus was trying to lift the consciousness of the Jewish people by teaching them the ability to resist the Roman Empire through passive resistance. For Thurman, Jesus's answer to those whose backs were against the wall was initially to realize the power within the self. He wrote that one tactic of imperialistic forces was to wage war on the consciousness of the individual through the use of segregation, taunts, and epithets aimed at creating a nihilistic psychology geared toward fearfulness and a feeling of inferiority. This tactic is put to rest through the Christian rhetoric of belonging to a Christian nation that had for its membership the very children of God. Also, to deal with the fear of dying, Christians were taught that death was not the end of the inner essence known as the soul. From this premise, it was easy for Christians to understand and to accept that no fear was due to those who could only kill the body.

This book of Thurman's, as the title *Jesus and the Disinherited* implies, is not just about the teachings of Jesus, but it is about how those teachings developed from the lived experience of a particular community, and it is also about how those teachings affected that community. Throughout the work, Thurman continues to keep in mind the comments and questions that gave impetus to the writing. He also kept in tension the community of which Jesus was a part with his own perception of the African American community and other oppressed communities of which he had knowledge. He saw a variety of similarities in all oppressed communities. Through the common term of oppression, Thurman is able to speak to the events in the individual communities; however, he is also able to transcend time and create a larger community of oppressed people who are now able to participate in the religion of Jesus regardless of their culture, nationality, or ethnicity. He does this by reducing the religion of Jesus to the simple but multileveled concept of love. Through this reduction, Thurman finds a defense for what he calls the three hounds of hell: fear, deception, and hate. This defense is simply to act based on love.

In 1954, Thurman was now the Dean of Marsh Chapel at Boston University. It was in this year that Thurman wrote an in-depth narrative about the nature of experiencing God, titled *The Creative Encounter*.[35] Thurman's stated purpose for the work was to study religious experience and its effect on the total life of the individual. The book was written in response to the growing tendency of scholars to concentrate on emotionless objective descriptions of their observations of the phenomenon of existence. It was in these descriptions that Thurman found inconsistencies with human reality. For Thurman, as God was Reality itself, to exist meant being fully immersed in God. In other words, in any observable phenomenon, if the individual is keenly aware, the presence of God can be realized. The beauty involved in this realization, according to Thurman, would make it impossible to give an emotionless response. This book is an attempt by one individual to account for the effect this type of encounter would have on the total life of an individual, both inner and outer.

Consciousness as a concept is used implicitly in this work. Religious experience is substituted for the concept of consciousness in the sense that it has been defined in this work as the awareness of a particular phenomenal reality, namely, the encounter with God. Religious experience, which for Thurman is considered to be a matter of fact of existence, assumes certain factors that are implicit in its description. Thurman describes the person experiencing the encounter as able to determine the nature of an otherwise unexplainable experience. Thurman also assumes that in every moment of people's existence, they are able to have this encounter if their sensibilities are heightened and they have little interference. This assumption is significant for the purpose of this research because the person's interpretation of his lived experience, which is inclusive of the creative encounter, will determine the person's perception of the outside world. Therefore, it is through the perception of the lived experience that the individual's subjective interpretation of reality is created, which in essence is consciousness. As this consciousness begins to be communicated socially, it is translated from individual consciousness to a communal or social consciousness. It functions by giving the individual a frame of reference from which to interpret the world; however, Thurman is very clear that the individual and his or her experiences are not the same. Individuals are the sole interpreters of their own life experiences, and therefore, they are able to become more than or less than the sum total of their experiences. What Thurman suggests here is that it is always the individual (not the encounter or the complete set of life's experiences) who determines the initial state of consciousness. Ultimately, there is a part of the individual that remains hidden from the world, and in this space, consciousness is born. It can be expanded but only as much or as little as the individual agrees.

This work is directed at the individual, but it has major implications for the community. Thurman focuses his energy on describing all aspects of the religious experience based on observations from his own. This direction of thought is displayed in the work prominently from its beginning. He states as a purpose for writing this work his concern for "the effect of religious experience upon the complete life of the individual."[36] This position helps him to defend his premise that once individuals intentionally choose to fully actualize their potential based on the experience of the creative encounter with God, then they become catalytic in the development process of the consciousness of the new community. Thurman refers to this intentional choice as a sacrifice unto the God of the creative encounter. After the initial sacrifice is made, the individual becomes conscious of a new world over and against the world that was experienced before the encounter. In this new world, the individual displays the catalytic behavior influenced by a strong desire to become God-like. With this new perspective, the individual now has to face the consequence of being transformed to a new consciousness in spite of living in an unchanged world. It is through this new consciousness that the individual realizes that if the fear of death can be transcended, then the unchanged world has no power. This is because for Thurman, the power obtained by the larger community through the threat of death to the individual causes many individuals to choose to protect their lives over giving themselves to some cause that might improve the community. When the individual has overcome this fear through an encounter with God, there is an overwhelming sense of love, according to Thurman. The result of receiving such a feeling of love causes them to desire and to seek love in their daily lives.

Thurman describes this process fully in the chapter on the outer necessity for love. First, the question is posed,

> Does the individual coming out of such a religious experience as defined make any impact on the cultural pattern which is his, and can the cultural pattern be so operated upon that it reflects the society in a manner that is favorable to the kind of religious experience discussed?[37]

Thurman describes several cultural patterns, the effect each had on the individual, and the individual's effect on the cultural pattern. Consequently, Thurman writes that the type of religious experience he previously described requires an individual-centered cultural pattern. In this cultural pattern, the individual is the major point of reference, meaning that the individual is the sole determinant in the creation of life's patterns. These patterns are founded on the individual's consciousness, which again is intentionally chosen from actualized potential based on life's experiences. In the individual-centered cultural pattern, individuals who have been transformed must now order their lives accordingly. To use a term from earlier, the social aesthete must now use the new insights gained through the creative encounter, which has changed his perception, to change the whole of his life. The creative encounter now becomes the basis for the development of the desired experience. Persons must spend their energies busying themselves no longer with self-actualization only but with community actualization so that the inner vision of what is possible becomes actual. As Thurman closes this work, he focuses on the visible manifestation of a social aesthete attempting to actualize such a social change. Although much of what Thurman describes takes place in the larger community, Thurman does intimate that a religious fellowship is most fulfilling to this sort of social aesthete, who is moved by a creative encounter with God, because in this fellowship, he can influence and be influenced by like-minded people.

Footprints of a Dream was written in 1959. It describes the founding of the Fellowship Church.[38] This book was intended to be the authoritative account of the historical background and an explanation of the purpose for the creation of the first interfaith, interracial religious body in the United States. It answers the question that Thurman had pondered since his experience of meeting Gandhi, where he was said to be a traitor to all people of color because he was a Christian. The Fellowship Church proved to Thurman and to the world that it was possible for people to join together in religious fellowship not because of ethnic or cultural heritage, but simply because of being like-minded or, in essence, having the same consciousness.

Consciousness was used implicitly in this work mainly to define the author's mindset and to also show how this mindset was used to create a certain consciousness among the group's members transforming the group into a community, which could then develop as an agent of change. The first chapter, titled "Khyber Pass," details the story of the events that led to Thurman's travels to India, Burma, and Ceylon. It was during this period that he visited the Khyber Pass, located on the northwest frontier of India. There, Thurman could stand and look over into Afghanistan, where he witnessed Muslims and Hindu people traveling on the same road bringing goods, culture, and their ideas along with them. Accordingly, it was in this epiphanic moment that he realized that this ancient, storied trade route cut across all religious and ethnic boundaries. It became his desire to prove to himself and the rest of the world that in Christianity lay the seeds with which to make this type of religious fellowship possible.

Throughout the remainder of the book, Thurman pays close attention to the historical significance of the church by describing the innovative programs, the commitment of the members, and the support this commitment elicited. He also took time to discuss the effect the church had on the immediate community and the community at large. In addition, he details at length how the church engaged in ensuring a certain culture was developed and a particular consciousness was maintained. However, in the final analysis, it is clear that Thurman's focus on the religion of Jesus is the ultimate reason for this development of culture and the maintenance of consciousness. To demonstrate this, he uses an interview method consisting of a questionnaire as the research tool. As a part of this research protocol, the following was one of the questions asked: "Have I observed any effect of the church on the community or persons who encounter it for the first time?" For this, he includes many more responses than he does for the other questions in the questionnaire. It is the conclusion of this researcher that Thurman did this because he considered this question to be more significant. Thurman appears devoted to the creation of community through the transformation of consciousness.

Footprints of a Dream demonstrates Thurman's belief that the Fellowship Church for All Peoples was not just a church, or a social movement, but it was both, and it firmly founded the belief that the religion of Jesus required community development and social transformation.

At a time when Thurman was beginning to reflect on his thoughts concerning the religion of Jesus, mysticism, experience, and community, he was asked to speak at the Rufus Jones Memorial Lectures. The reason he was chosen to speak was that by this time, he was gaining notoriety for the founding of the Fellowship Church, and also he had written six books, which included three books of sermons and meditations. He was also deferent to the fact that he had studied with Rufus Jones in 1929, and that this study helped him to express his ideas aloud concerning the relationship of humans with God. The lecture took place in 1961, and Thurman published the lecture later the same year, after some revision, under the title "Mysticism and the Experience of Love."[39] Much earlier, in 1939, Thurman spoke at Eden Theological Seminary, where he gave a total of four lectures under the title of "Mysticism and Social Change."[40] In these lectures, he tied the inward desire to experience God with the public responsibility to challenge those things that hindered that experience for him and others. The 1961 lecture serves as an addendum to the earlier lectures by calling attention to the necessity of creating a private life despite the mystic's public responsibility to become involved in the attempt to transform the social order and eliminate social despair. In this work, Thurman focuses on those conscious moments with the holy that can be gained during the inward journey of the private life.

Consciousness is used in this work explicitly as Thurman defines mysticism through the writings of Rufus Jones. According to Jones, "mysticism is used to express the type of religion which puts the emphasis on the immediate awareness of a relationship with God, on direct and intimate consciousness of the Divine Presence."[41] This definition qualifies as a direct use of the term consciousness, which was defined earlier as knowledge of a specific phenomenal event. After putting forth this definition, Thurman begins to use the term mysticism among others to speak of a particular type of consciousness, which is knowledge of God. His purpose for using the term in this manner is to instruct his audience of the detrimental effect that reduction of the private life was having on the ability to have the mystic experience. Thurman writes, "Togetherness is becoming the watch-word of our times. It seems that it is more and more a substitute for God."[42] For Thurman, it was more important for the individual to have the space within which to find the connection to God which lies in every person. After traveling along the inward journey and finding this connection, the individual can then form community with other fellow travelers who have had this mystic experience. If individuals are able to find this connecting point within, then they will be able to order their lives according to their new found inner consciousness as opposed to being outer-directed by what Thurman calls the "Grand Invasion."[43] Not being outer-directed became significantly important for Thurman; he describes his experience of being forced to live in a segregated American society as having made it urgently necessary to seek "a means for sustaining the personal enterprise of [his] life beyond all of the ravages inflicted upon it by the brutalities of the social order."[44] The consciousness gained from the mystic experience, or the direct relationship with God through intentionally focusing on his presence in everyday life, gave Thurman the ability to rise above the outer life experience of being subjected to racial oppression.

Furthermore, the book was written with a double intention of making both the individual and the mystic community, a community formed through the relationship of individuals having had or seeking the mystic experience, realize that the "mystic's object is God."[45] Thurman accomplishes this purpose by focusing his line of thought toward the necessities of the mystic's experience. He does this by first describing the mystic's lived experience and also the desired experience. The lived experience is the overwhelming feeling the individual has as a result of being encroached by outside life. He gives an example of standing in an intersection that is so noisy that the individual has a difficult time determining the nature of any sound in particular. The individual must intentionally focus on particular individual sounds to distinguish any distinct sound. He intentionally describes focusing in this manner as a process of "centering down." In the process of centering down, if the mystic has a vision of the purposes of God and responds to this vision, then the mystic has participated in the purposes of God. This response makes the mystic an aesthete by the definition used in this research because the mystic now has a high admiration of the beauty that is found in the vision of God's purpose.

Thurman refers to this relationship between the mystic and the purposes of God as the experience of love. This love is felt by the mystic at the center of his being, and it is the desire of the mystic to feel this love in the lived community of men. This becomes the desired experience. The mystic desires to share this experience of love with all and, according to Thurman, seeks out ways to make this possible. This desire to share the experience of love with all is not limited to the human community. It is open to all of creation. The mystic's perception is now changed, which in turn causes an inner and outer change in the mystic. This change causes some mystics to retreat into solitariness and others to strive for the manifestation of their vision in their everyday lives. Of this, Thurman writes, "any structure of society, any arrangement under which human beings live that does not provide for the maximum opportunities for free flowing and circulation among each other, works against individual and social health."[46] This statement demonstrates the type of community Thurman envisioned when he co-founded the Fellowship Church. It also speaks to the type of political stance on social transformation in the wider community. Thurman insists that segregating communities according to race, or any other factor, stifles the love ethic and creates bad social health. This phenomenon also hinders the experience of love.

In the next book to be examined, *Disciplines of the Spirit*, Thurman gives space to the instruction of how the individual can become intently focused on building this stronger relationship with the Holy. In the foreword, he announces that it is his intent to examine certain aspects of the human experience, focusing on those that have the ability to tutor the human spirit. This book arises from the sermons and many courses that Thurman taught while at Boston University. It was during this period that the focus of Thurman's teachings centered on the growth and the strengthening of the spirit through rigorous spiritual discipline. For Thurman, this strengthening took shape within a religious context, with the end result being the merging of the individual spirit into full consciousness of the presence and the oneness of God's spirit. This process would manifest itself in the physical world as an elevated communal relationship among humans.

In many of Thurman's writings, including this one, the idea of the spirit is enveloped within the idea of consciousness. The two become one in such a way that for Thurman's purposes, consciousness is representative of all of human consciousness; however, he does create space for the role that the lived experience plays in shaping consciousness. He does this also with experience, by speaking of conscious experience as if it were one with unconscious experience and can be known in much the same way. In this framework, Thurman is able to speak about the ability to train spirit and allow this to include the training of the thinking and the deep emotional consciousness that each individual has. This is important because, from this point of view, the whole of the book is about consciousness, and it grows from Thurman's understanding that lack of growth of the spirit hinders our individual actualization and that of the world. This means that weak spirits keep the world from becoming what it could be. With that in mind, this book becomes not just a work about bettering the individual's relationship with God, but it also brings along with this idea the concept of how to make a better world through the bettering of all individuals' spirit.

Disciplines of the Spirit begins with a discussion about commitment, which is practically synonymous with intentionality. His usage of commitment in connection to spirit is almost identical to the way in which Husserl, the father of the phenomenological movement, sought to explain Being through practical descriptions of what it meant to be conscious. As consciousness is always of something, so too is the spirit—committed to something, even if, in fact, it is to nothingness. Of commitment Thurman writes,

> It has been wisely said that the time and the place of man's life on earth is the time and the place of his body, but the meaning of his life is as significant and eternal as he wills to make. While he is on earth, his mind and spirit are domiciled in his body, bound up in a creature who is at once a child of nature and of God. Commitment means that is possible for a man to yield the nerve center of his consent to a purpose or cause, a movement or an ideal, which may be more important to him than whether his lives or dies.[47]

Here, Thurman adds another characteristic of what it means to be committed. Committed simply means focused on something conceived in the mind or perceived through the senses. Thurman connects the body as well as the mind in a way that changes the person forever, because now this focus has become a calling. The person's consciousness changes his or her perspective so much that the person changes himself or herself even physically to meet the challenge, that is, athletes, dancers, and soldiers. The significance of this line of thought in Thurman's writings is multileveled. On one level, it shows that Thurman understood the necessity of dealing with the mind/body problem of philosophy, which by this period had become interwoven into religious interpretation. Many Christian theologians and parishioners were interpreting Christianity to the world as a religion concerned with only the spiritual and not the physical. Thurman is clearly addressing worldly and extraworldly concerns. On an even different level, this line of thought shows Thurman's knowledge of such thinkers as John Dewey and Martin Heidegger. Thurman was not just an articulate minister, but he was also an intellect who could toil with difficult ideas and synthesize them into usable pieces of information for his congregants and his students.

This book has many implications for the individual and also for the community interested in transformation. Although it focuses on the transition of the United States during the interim period after the passing of the 1954 legislation striking down legal segregation, Thurman recognized that for the true transformation of any population where extreme psychological barriers have been in place, a shift in the consciousness of the people is necessary in order that a real community may be formed. This type of society built on the new or renewed consciousness holds within it the ability for all individuals to actualize their fullest potential. For Thurman, the fullest potential was for all individuals to assimilate the characteristics of the divine in all aspects of life. Thurman believed that this type of community was possible; however, American society would need to be taught the ability to discipline the spirit, so that it would be prepared for the sharing of the mystic vision. This mystic vision would carry the possibility for a new aesthetic on which this new community could now be built. That is to say, the perceptions of Americans would be altered in a way that would reduce the individual's ability to experience pleasure in a society that institutionalized oppression.

In examining Thurman's direction of thought, two concepts become prominent outside of the religion of Jesus and mysticism. Consciousness and race become very intertwined throughout Thurman's writings. So much so, that it is very difficult to consider Thurman's thought concerning his definition of Being without considering the ramifications that race added to his description. Thurman realizes that to bring about the type of change he was able to effect in San Francisco, a transformation of the nation's attitude toward race had to occur. In *The Luminous Darkness*, Thurman describes the hindrances of racial segregation in terms of a nation's ability to create the unity apparent in his philosophical vision.[48] According to him, unity was the central purpose of religious experience. It was what he dedicated his life to bringing to pass. In order that this might come to pass, he believed that a change in consciousness had to take place for whites and for blacks so that they could live together in community. However, the kind of change that had to take place or from what frame of reference was dependent on the experience or idiom of that particular race.

In *The Luminous Darkness*, Thurman makes use of a style of philosophical reasoning that was created by phenomenological thinkers in an attempt to describe what Being is. The major question of phenomenology has to do the essence of Being. In this philosophical movement, there are many major proponents; however, Edmund Husserl and Martin Heidegger are two of the most important: Husserl is usually thought as the progenitor of the philosophy, and Heidegger was a student of Husserl. As for phenomenology's importance in this research, Thurman makes great strides at putting forth his understanding of what it means to be human by intentionally focusing on the pervasive nature of racism through the vehicle of segregation. He accomplishes this task by admitting that racism had so infected all of American life, particularly in the South, that there could be no way to describe the phenomenon of being alive without making reference directly to racism or discussing its effects. In fact, when Thurman describes segregation, it can be taken for granted that he is philosophically describing what it means to "be" during this period.

As this description pertains to consciousness, there can be no consciousness outside the reality of racism. For Thurman, the only way one could remain in a racist society and describe Being, absent of the knowledge of racism, was to suspend any knowledge of racism, as it pertained to any description of Being. Being, for him, was incarnated within the black world of family and friends. The interactions with whites were something indescribably different. It was outside the realm of reality.[49] Normal time and space relationships did not apply. In this definition, the knower intentionally has knowledge of phenomena. The phenomenon being known does not change based on the knower; however, the description changes based on the knower's perception. In many cases, blacks and whites chose to compartmentalize their lives so as not to allow the racist treatment to become a part of their self-estimate. This was especially true when blacks were trying to determine the ethics of a situation. Racism was so prevalent that it was not factored into ethical discourse. It was as if racism were as invisible as the air which we take for granted.

Consciousness and the need for a change in consciousness are dealt with explicitly in the text. Thurman uses consciousness as a basis from which to make his main point—namely, that racism in the form of segregation has hurt the psyche of whites and blacks so profoundly that humanness has a hard time being displayed. Accordingly, both racial groups have regressed in their behavior so much that without a change of consciousness, social transformation will not occur by just removing the wall of segregation. Thurman writes, "The burden of being black and the burden of being white is so heavy that it is rare in our society to experience oneself as human."[50] It is evident through Thurman's treatment of the experience of blacks and whites that he is at least partially convinced that the most detrimental effect of racism on the American society has been the damage done to the national self-consciousness and that this damage is pronounced in the treatment and the reaction to the treatment. Thurman appears convinced that the solution to this problem is to create a God consciousness in the greater American community, much the same as was implemented at the Fellowship Church.

This work is directed to the public at large. At this time, Thurman had become a senior advisor to both the black community and wider public of all Americans. He had retired and had decided that he must make space in his journey to become a public intellectual with the audacity to speak to all Americans critically. Consequently, *The Luminous Darkness* is written from the standpoint of an authority figure who has now earned the right to say what he does to all people based on his life's experience and employment adventures. This work focuses on what types of changes the society had to make after desegregation if America was to achieve in reality that which it had already claimed figuratively through declarations, historical legal precedent, and even in its anthem. The book also urges action on the part of individuals to first change their personal ethic and then to work toward forming community. For Thurman, community development and social transformation began with the individual's consciousness. Thurman believed that the essence of community was born in the individual through his relationship or lack thereof with the holy. It was then necessary for the individual to intentionally attempt to focus on strengthening this primary relationship before the secondary outer relationship could have the ability to transform. Of the several statements made by Thurman that point to his intent, the following seems to capture the whole of his thought on the matter:

> It may be that the experience of which we speak is not possible unless and until the individual sees himself as a being contained or held something so much more than he is that his life is brought into focus of self-conscious meaning and value. Such an experience is possible only in the light of ultimate values and ultimate meanings. And this is what religion undertakes to guarantee; the extent to which it would guarantee such an experience for the individual.[51]

In the next work to be examined, *The Search for Common Ground*, Thurman attempts to bring all of his life's experiences and writings together in one volume to answer the following question: if we know all life is one, how do humans live together as though we know this to be true?[52] He begins this work by pondering lifelong questions he had asked in the midst of a period in American history marred by social unrest and a call by certain black leaders for blacks to separate from whites. At first, it appears that he is simply asking, "Is there a God that we are connected to ancestrally, and through which we have the ability, if not the desire, to live in community?" However, to think of Thurman's lifelong quest in these terms is a major oversimplification. This type of reading of Thurman's works creates an unintended disconnect that is problematic when charting his aim over time and leads to the omission of Thurman's name when considering philosophical and theological subjects such as ontology and cosmology.

Community is a subject of extreme significance in the writings of Thurman. This much is well documented; however, very little has been said about his search for common ground, which is over and above his desire for community. Common ground for him is the cause of any desire toward community in all living beings but specifically humans. It is because of his conception of common ground that he is drawn into the indirect discussion of separation not being a viable option for blacks. This conception brings about the realization that this type of separation stymies the development of the highest levels of community that he is convinced humans can achieve. Community is referred to in this work as "realized potential."[53] Without this level of development, human individuals are unable to actualize their highest potential.

In the first chapter of the book, Thurman begins with a discussion about the interdependence of life. Through this discussion, he outlines the premise for his major claim of what he refers to as common ground. He writes, "Life feeds on life; life is nourished by life. It is life's experience with itself that establishes the ground for the dogma that life is eternal."[54] For him, life becomes the common entity that forms the connection between all living things. They are connected in the fact that they are living organisms, and as such, they share certain common characteristics, that is, responding to the environment, change, and the need for some energy source. However, Thurman takes this common connection a step further by making the claim that life itself is alive. He also takes this premise further by referring to life as also being conscious. He acknowledges this claim as follows: " . . . the intent of creation is that life lives by constantly seeking to realize itself in established forms, patterns and units."[55] To speak of life and the creation as acting in an intentional manner is to ascribe to life the quality of consciousness. When he speaks of life in this manner, he is basically claiming that we not only desire community because we share a common quality, which is life, but that we share life itself, because, for Thurman, all life is one.

Thurman's explanation of the interdependence of life also has a religious basis in that Thurman equates the mind of God with existence. Of this Thurman writes,

> The religious basis for such an interpretation of community is the affirmation, which to me is categorical, that the Mind of God is realizing Itself in time, and that there are observable patterns or sequences in all creation . . . all things, even existence itself, are regarded as the mind of God coming to Itself in time and space.[56]

Thurman wrote of creation as being alive and equating to the Mind of God because of the patterns that he observed. The repetitious nature of these patterns indicated intelligence and a certain quality called rhythm.

The acknowledgment of this rhythm is part of the mystic experience for him. This can be thought of in much the same way as the aesthetic experience for John Dewey.[57] The aesthetic experience, as John Dewey explains, is when the perceiver takes part in the creation over and above mere recognition. He explains that perception differs from recognition because perception brings reception to fulfillment. The perceiver mentally recreates in much the same way that the original creation is organized. It is an ordering of the parts so that a complete form is then established. For Thurman, to take notice of the existing patterns or forms is to place the individual elements of each form into a specific order (i.e., a community). This must be done through mental re-creation in much the same way that the existing patterns were created initially to have a perception of the patterns. This perception creates a particular type of experience for the perceiver, which, according to Thurman, is the mystic experience. From this point of view, it necessarily followed that community was an inevitable part of existence and that wherever community did not exist, two antithetical characteristics would appear—conflict and the desire for community. This also helps explain why Thurman considered anything destroying the communal bound as sinful.

The phenomenon of the communal rhythm in existence is thought to be intentional through the dynamic intelligence behind the creation, which again for Thurman is the mind of God. He was clear, however, that to speak of this creative intelligence in this manner was to anthropomorphize, which is why he borrows other nomenclature such as the undifferentiated aesthetic continuum.[58] This communal rhythm is where the discussion concerning the seeker of community begins. He can be described as a social aesthete, or one who desires to recreate a particular aesthetic experience individually and for others, which involves the mental act of perception. The absence of this experience is described as chaotic and opposed to life. So the mystic, who is now the social aesthete of the mystic experience, is one seeking to bring order out of a perceived chaotic moment. To perform this task, the mystic moves according to the perception that is now imprinted in the mystic's consciousness. In regard to this Thurman writes, "In the conflicts between man and man, between group and group, between nation and nation, the loneliness of the seeker for community is sometimes unendurable."[59]

Consciousness is used in this work explicitly as a means by which communication takes place between existence and its many forms. For Thurman, it is the mystic who is able to take notice of this experience at a higher level, because the spiritual disciplines the mystic has performed clear much of the noise of everyday life away, creating for the mystic a keener perception. He also dedicates a chapter in this work to the discussion of common consciousness. In this chapter, the case is made for the possibility of interspecies and intra-species communication. He quickly moves from this discussion to what he calls the more obvious communication between members of the same species or family. He argues that this communication is not, as it may seem, the communication between individuals, but it is the communication of life which itself in each form and therefore this communication is one. Thurman refers to this phenomenon as the activity of a singular organism. Within species, this activity is called community. Accordingly, communication can be said to be an intentional effort or conscious attempt on the part of life to survive. This is done through the sharing of consciousness, or also for what John Searle refers to as collective intentionality.[60]

This work targets communities as a whole, but specifically the black community. The work was written in the aftermath of the Martin Luther King assassination. Then, as well as throughout the turbulent 1960s, there were calls for the separation of the black and white races. Separation was considered by Thurman to be the ultimate denial of the true nature of God. His intent was that anyone reading *The Search for Common Ground* would clearly understand that the need and desire for community were as much a part of humanity as was life. Accordingly, community development and social transformation will take place if nothing happens to hinder the natural order of things. He does not address whether or not hindrances are inevitable. However, he does seem to imply that the possibility is at least always there to have hindrances as he writes,

> The notion that a man is the higher animal and all the others are lower, the development of elaborate self-consciousness in man, the ability to think reflectively that is a use of the mind that gives it the sense of living its own life apart from the body—all of these and kindred ideas have erected a great wall between man and other animals. The sense of separateness from the rest of nature is so marked that man tends see himself as being over and against nature.

In defense of this conceit, various dogmas and even theologies have been developed. My point is not absolute. Life is always seeking to realize itself in myriad forms and patterns of manifestation. These forms and consciousness or awareness are life at its most elemental level and self-consciousness in its profoundest expression.[61]

Thurman provides a major implication for community development and social transformation through his work, which suggests that shared communal consciousness is possible based on his belief that life is one. Quite simply, therefore, humans actualize their highest potential always in community and never in isolation.

NOTES

1 Howard Thurman, *The Mood at Christmas Time* (New York: Harper & Row), 10.

2 Howard Thurman, *Mysticism and the Experience of Love* (Wallingford, PA: Pendle Hill, 1961), 6.

3 Howard Thurman, *With Head and Heart: The Autobiography of Howard Thurman* (San Diego: Harcourt Brace Jovanovich, 1981), 29.

4 Ibid.

5 Thurman, Fluker, and Tumber, *Strange Freedom*, 103 (see chap. 2, n. 4).

6 Ibid.

7 Ibid.

8 Luther E. Smith Jr., *Howard Thurman: Essential Writings, Modern Spiritual Master Series* (Maryknoll, NY: Orbis Books, 2006), 45.

9 Smith, *Mystic as Prophet*, 45–48 (see chap. 1, n. 6).

10 Thurman, Fluker, and Tumber, *Strange Freedom*, 110 (see chap. 2, n. 4).

11 Ibid., 114.

12 Smith, *Howard Thurman: Essential Writings*, 14.

13 Howard Thurman, *The Luminous Darkness: A Personal Interpretation of the Anatomy of Segregation and the Ground of Hope* (New York: Harper & Row, 1965), x.

14 Thurman, *With Head and Heart*, 4.

15 Thurman, Fluker, and Tumber, *Strange Freedom*, 104 (see chap. 2, n. 4).

16 Ibid.

17 Thurman, Fluker, and Tumber, *Strange Freedom*, 111 (see chap. 2, n. 4).

18 Howard Thurman and Walter E. Fluker, *The Papers of Howard Washington Thurman* (Columbia: University of South Carolina Press, 2009), 110.

19 Ibid.

20 Ibid.

21 Thurman, *Jesus and the Disinherited*, 29 (see chap. 1, n. 24).

22 Thurman, *With Head and Heart*, 132.

23 Howard Thurman, *Deep River and the Negro Spiritual Speaks of Life and Death* (Richmond: Friends United Press, 1975), 3–4.
24 Ibid., 11.
25 Ibid., 39.
26 Ibid.
27 Ibid., 17.
28 Ibid., 56.
29 Thurman, *Jesus and the Disinherited*, 7–8 (see chap. 1, n. 24).
30 Ibid., 15.
31 Ibid.
32 KJV Matthew 5:41–42.
33 Thurman, *Jesus and the Disinherited*, 49 (see chap. 1, n. 24).
34 Ibid.
35 Howard Thurman, *The Creative Encounter: An Interpretation of Religion and the Social Witness* (New York: Harper, 1954), 7–8.
36 Ibid., 10.
37 Ibid., 125.
38 Howard Thurman, *Footprints of a Dream: The Story of the Church for the Fellowship of All Peoples* (New York: Harper, 1959), 7–9.
38 Thurman, *Mysticism and the Experience of Love*, 3.
40 Ibid.
41 Ibid., 6.
42 Ibid., 4.
43 Ibid.
44 Ibid., 5.
45 Ibid., 9.
46 Ibid., 19.
47 Howard Thurman, *Disciplines of the Spirit* (New York: Harper & Row, 1963), 17.
48 Thurman, *Luminous Darkness*, ix–x.
49 Ibid., 2–5.
50 Ibid., 94.
51 Ibid., 101.
52 Thurman, *Search for Common Ground*, 4–7 (see chap. 1, n. 4).
53 Ibid., 5.
54 Ibid., 4.
55 Ibid.
56 Ibid., 5.
57 Dewey, *Art as Experience*, 54 (see chap. 2, n. 25).
58 Thurman, *Search for Common Ground*, 6 (see chap. 1, n. 4).
59 Ibid.
60 John R. Searle, *The Construction of Social Reality* (New York: Free Press, 1995), 23.
61 Ibid., 63.

4

NEWTON'S KNOWLEDGE-SHAPING EXPERIENCES

The communications revolution, combined with the expansive domination of the American empire, has created the "global village."
—Huey P. Newton

Huey P. Newton was as an activist whose scholarly writings and public activities demonstrate the basic foundational creed of his philosophy, which was "revolutionary suicide." His writings seem to foreshadow his eventual, but untimely demise. The very idea that his philosophical understanding of revolution focuses on the type of death the revolutionary will experience preempts the fact that death as a result of his own actions would be his end. However, despite the profundity of the work and activity in which Huey Newton was involved, there is, with the exception of a few institutions, a great void in academia where he is concerned. This void can be attributed mainly to the antagonistic and revolutionary stance Newton and the Black Panthers took toward the United States government and the white-dominated capitalistic economic structure.

In Newton's doctoral dissertation, it is recounted that J. Edgar Hoover mandated that the purpose of Counter Intelligence Program (COINTEL-PRO) be to prevent the rise of another black messiah. Also, Hoover and the Federal Bureau of Investigation (FBI) along with COINTELPRO shifted their focus from Martin Luther King and other leaders to the Black Panther Party and Huey P. Newton because Hoover believed the Panthers were the biggest threat to internal security in the nation. Much of this fear had to do with the Panthers' belief in self-defense. In fact, much of what is known about Newton leaves most individuals considering him to be a rifle-carrying, black hoodlum wearing a black beret and leather jacket. To simply describe him in this manner is a demonstration of how badly a deeper and more objective study is needed.

Robert Trivers is currently an expert in evolutionary biology working at Rutgers. Trivers is said to be the inspiration behind the works of Richard Dawkins and Edward O. Wilson, who are themselves acclaimed biologists. Trivers met Newton in 1972 and they worked on several papers researching consciousness, deceit, and self-deception. Their most notable work is an analysis of the victims from a plane crash titled, "The Crash of Air Florida Flight 90." Trivers wrote in his recently released papers that "Newton was one of five or six geniuses I met in my lifetime."[1] He also said that "Newton's logic was well above average."[2] Erik Erikson compared Newton with Gandhi in the way that Newton was able to cause a transvaluation of images in the consciousness of the people.[3] Erikson would also call this a psychic transformation. Although Newton did believe that violence would be necessary to protect the black community from the aggressive tactics of police brutality, to describe Newton as an armed leather jacket wearing hooligan is to ignore the totality of his life.

In Newton's book co-authored with Erik Erikson titled *In Search for Common Ground*, Erikson referred to Newton as a radical theorist.[4] Judson Jeffries, in *Huey Newton: The Radical Theorist*, outlined Newton's social/political thought.[5] In this chapter, the root metaphor "radical theorist"[6] will be analyzed to see if in fact it is an accurate description for Newton. To best accomplish this task, after defining the term, Newton's theories will be analyzed historically in context with other social and political theorists to substantiate the claim that Newton was a theorist with a radical nature.

The word "theory" originated from a Greek term, *theorein*, which meant to look at, to behold, and to contemplate. In other words, when an individual intentionally examines a phenomenon with the aim of forming a reasoned explanation, the individual has engaged in the creation of a theory. This process has taken place formally and informally since the dawning of human consciousness. Theories have been formed to explain a vast array of phenomena spanning all human activity. What defines a political theorist as opposed to other theorists is that political theorists provide a "way of looking at politics which adds up to a symbolic picture of an ordered whole."[7] These theorists are also distinguished from others by the fact that they possess a vision that they believe to be an explanation of how the politics of the world in which we live should operate.

There are many examples of political theory that vary from the extremely intricate and complicated to simple theories that demonstrate a lack of logical, political, or social analysis. Political theorists often are focused on forming theories that create fertile ground for the existence of the good life within a community. In doing so, certain questions or ideas have become recurring themes within the study of political life. Some of these questions are "What are the natural standards of justice?," "Who should be entrusted with power?," and "In what way can the state contribute to human freedom and in what ways must the state constrain human freedom?" Such questions are aimed at the expression of what the good society is. Historically, the classical body of literature associated with political theory is thought to contain these theories created by Plato, Aristotle, and others who formed their theories during the classical period of Greece. Although these theories have many areas in which they diverge, there are similarities that are believed to lay the foundation for all the subsequent political theories.

Reason or its usage is considered the connecting strand of all classical philosophy. Reason as a guide to directing the future and interpreting events of the past is thought to have originated during the classical period in Greece. This is significant because many Greek philosophers pay homage to Egypt for their education. However, many classical Greek scholars consider the Greek philosophers to have separated themselves from their Egyptian education by not relying on the "Gods" for the answers to questions that they believed could give direction in attaining the good life. Reason's central test of validity is to ask the question, "how does one know if the premises one's ideas are based upon are true." This question or a similar version forms the fundamental framework for all philosophical thought. It is the basic tool that allows for the forming of a conclusion or shaping of judgments, which is the staple activity of all classical philosophy. Political visions over time would depart from the classical theory in content, but they would not depart from the basic framework. Each theorist used the above-mentioned method to address the problems or contradictions in their own community. The use of the common method is what denotes whether the mental exercise engaged in is the creation of theory in the classical meaning of the word.

RADICAL THEORIST

Many black social theorists are thought to rely on rhetoric as opposed to creatively constructing a social reality based on material fact. The use of reason by Huey Newton to rationally answer the immediate and long-range problems that plagued his community allows for his inclusion among the fraternity of visionary political thinkers. His thoughts concerning his vision of a community were examined in detail by Judson Jeffries, who titled his book, *Huey P. Newton: The Radical Theorist*, a root metaphor given to Newton by Erik Erikson during their 1971 talks.[8] According to Jeffries, Newton can be considered alongside such theorists as Hobbes, Locke, Rousseau, and Marx. In Jeffries's description of Newton's political vision, five major categories can be identified along with several sub-categories. The major categories are citizenry, community, laws, economics, and the state.

Just as other major theorists before him, Newton includes his observation of basic human nature in his theoretical portrait of society. He opines that individuals are generally motivated by personal desire. He bases this presumption on the environment in which he lived and his reading of such writers as Hobbes and Nietzsche. For Newton, the struggle to be free was innate to being human. He disagreed with Martin Luther King that freedom for African Americans comes from being morally good. For Newton, it was social oppression which restricted freedom, and to struggle against oppression of any type was a prelude to freedom, which also had the benefit of restoring spiritual dignity to the individual. To explain this position, Newton uses a suicide analogy in which two profiles are employed. The first profile is given the name reactionary suicide. He describes reactionary suicide as a reaction to social conditions in which the individual commits suicide due to the overwhelming feeling of hopelessness and helplessness. Revolutionary suicide, on the contrary, is when the individual is so committed to the idea of personal individual freedom that he is willing to sacrifice his life for it. According to Newton, it is better to oppose forces that would drive one to self-murder than to endure them. For him, the highest form of a demonstrated innate desire for freedom is to engage in revolutionary suicide.

For Newton, African Americans as a community desired freedom the same as any community; however, it was fear which prohibited any forward steps toward this goal. Fear, for Newton, was a weapon of the oppressor, which was important because of its residual effect. It would be necessary, according to Newton, for blacks to pass through fear to experience liberation. The type of fear that Newton is describing has little to do with emotions attached to an upcoming event or situation. This fear has more to do with the memory associated with the effect of a community's response to oppression. In fact, for Newton, this very foundation on which a community is built is a shared consciousness stemming in part from the cultural memory that shapes the present and future culture. Newton was fully aware of how important culture was in shaping the consciousness of a community. The Black Panthers were created with the idea that if the consciousness of the community was raised, causing a realization of the cause of their fear, then the culture of fear could be altered to a revolutionary culture focused on the destruction of all oppression. This ideal conception was put into action through the many survival programs initiated by the Panthers. This series of collective sacrificial actions were revolutionary in that they gave the community the ability to provide services for themselves, which allowed for the community to realize that they had the ability to exist independently of what the government provided. From this realization, it was now a relatively simple leap of logic to see that not only was the desire to be free innate but also the tools that could make this realizable were innate.

Although Newton was engaged in actions that could be viewed as an attempt to undermine the state's control over its citizenry, he was convinced of the state's right to make laws that its citizens must follow—at least, if the laws served the people. For him, these laws should enhance civil society and not hinder or oppress it, by improving the general welfare of the people. According to Jeffries, it is easy to see the effect that the writings of John Locke had on Newton. Newton and Locke both subscribed to the idea that a basic right of the people is to change laws that do not concern their best interest. Locke's pragmatic stance on the government led him to posit the idea that people should remove any part of the government when they find that it acts contrary to the trust given to it. Economics also plays into Newton's vision of the state in much the same way as it did in the vision of Marx. Because of Newton's communalist stance, those in control of the means of production are obligated to use their assets for the benefit of the whole community. For him, the state must protect the lives, rights, and property of the whole community and not just the ruling class. The end of classes, for Newton (as for Marx), is the ultimate goal.

Newton, according to Matthew W. Hughey, "attempted to reinstall Enlightenment values of reason and freedom into modern discourse which aimed at pragmatic consensus."[9] He put forth his vision of a state and its relationship to its citizens based on a well-reasoned solution to the contradictions he experienced in society. Although his political theory shared many similarities with other theories considered to be more classical, his theory was also considered to be radical. It was important for Newton that the solutions that he addressed to the problem of oppression in his community were applicable within a specific amount of time and not merely popular. He recognized that ineffective popular solutions (such as various back to Africa movements) had plagued blacks for centuries. He was also aware that oppression had tentacles that affected the black community in diverse ways. Many groups whose aim was to alleviate the painful life caused by oppression oftentimes only reacted passively to these oppressive tentacles. Newton realized that as the oppression was evolving, being merely reactive would never work, and therefore, any plan of action needed to be revolutionary and not reactive. To accomplish this goal, it would take reason to devise a plan that took into account the communal experience, and then devise strategies addressing the total problem by examining the historical and philosophical causes.

Newton called his political theory "Revolutionary Intercommunalism." Intercommunalism, according to Newton, was based on the premise that the nations of the world had evolved into communities. He defined a community as a small unit with a comprehensive collection of institutions that exist to serve a small group of people. He saw these communities as being controlled by a small circle of individuals who profited from hegemonic structures such as the European and American capitalistic alliance. Revolutionary intercommunalism sought to create egalitarianism among community members by raising the consciousness of the masses, allowing them to see their connection to the worldwide oppressed community. Newton felt that through this knowledge of a common source of oppression, coalitions would be formed. The coalitions would work to seize power and the sources of wealth. They would then work toward the shifting of power from the few to the masses. This type of transition is more than a radical notion. Self-determination, economic determination, and cultural determination, which were formerly controlled by the small ruling circle, would now be in the hands of the masses. This is why Newton's theory is radical.

EXPERIENCE

When considering the events that led to the founding of the Black Panther Party, it is necessary to consider the inevitability of its appearance as a driving force in the development of the consciousness of Huey Newton. Frustration and contradiction characterized much of black life, especially in U.S. cities. Many blacks were not satisfied with the approaches used by leaders who were convinced that nonviolence was the only way blacks could solve their problems of oppression and remain human. The more violence was used as an instrument of oppression, the more inner city blacks became disenchanted with nonviolent strategies. This became the recipe from which flowed the sentiment that self-defense was not only moral but also necessary. Those who experienced the violent weapon of oppression became predisposed toward taking a militant defensive posture. This posture is what led to the founding of groups such as the Black Panther Party.

Newton, like many of his contemporaries, was given to such a defensive posture because of his particular experiences and, more specifically, his perception of those experiences. Early in Newton's life, he was a self-described seeker. It was the contradiction of everyday black life that frustrated and also confused him, causing him to retreat into activities that were considered anti-establishment. These activities were a response to his inner desire to break free from a racially oppressive environment containing few options for upward social mobility. About this, he writes, "About two years before I completed high school, my inner life was plunged into a sea of confusion and turmoil that lasted until Bobby Seale and I organized the Black Panther Party."[10] Newton also attempted to put into perspective the contrasting lifestyles of his two older brothers, Sonny Man and Melvin. For Newton, each of his brothers represented lifestyles with trajectories aimed at contrasting modes of freedom. Melvin was a graduate student and also an adjunct professor, and Sonny Man was a common street hustler. Both lifestyles held some complexities. Sonny Man's lifestyle, while appealing because of the freedom it provided, answered none of the questions about existence, which puzzled Newton and drove him to be a seeker. Melvin, on the contrary, was an academic; however, Newton's level of reading would have to greatly increase in order for him to appreciate the pathway of this brother.

After co-founding the Black Panther Party, Newton's life changed drastically. He immediately went from being a part-time student and hustler to a nationally recognized antagonist to America's majority way of life. Immediately after Friday, October 27, 1967, which was the night Officer Frey was shot allegedly by Newton, a Free Huey campaign gave popularity to Huey and the Black Panther Party beyond all of the founders' expectations. Newton was described as the embodiment of resistance for a generation. Ironically, he was neither a gifted nor enthusiastic speaker, but he was considered to be the leader of a group of very dynamic speakers. This group of dynamic speakers was able to mobilize members of the Black Panther Party during the period of Newton's incarceration from October 1967 to August 1970.

UNSHAVEN BEATNIK

How does an individual transition from being described by his siblings as being too pretty for a boy when he was very young to being considered the major catalyst of a movement populated with low-life, gun-carrying, black beret-wearing hoodlums? Much of the credit for this characterization can be given to the times that created Newton. In 1964, the Civil Rights Act was signed.[11] The next year, after Lyndon Johnson gave his celebrated "Great Society" speech, the Watts Rebellion took place. Within the next two years, there were over a hundred major race-related riots across the country. The escalation of the Vietnam War also served to stir up emotions among a nation of youth already agitated by the racial tensions. This environment nurtured Huey Newton into a defiant personality.

This defiance began while Newton was still living at home with his parents. As stated earlier, he was a self-professed seeker, searching for his own identity over and against that which the society forced on him, intellectually, spiritually, and physically. It is apparent that he was struggling to forge his own individuality despite the fact that he was a member of an ethnic group that suffered from severe social isolation. Human identity is defined by the awareness of individual uniqueness as well as awareness of the commonality shared with a group.[12] Newton lived during a period in the nation's history when both identities were restricted by oppressive obstacles. Consequently, he felt a strong need to assert that these obstacles would not be tolerated any more. He was now compatible with the classic definition of a rebel. It was now his time to do what he believed he had a right to do.

In the fall of 1959, Newton began taking classes at Oakland City College. Continuing to search for identity, he fell in with the beatnik crowd, and grew a beard. This became a source of contention with his parents because they felt as if he were throwing away the values they tried to instill in him. His father insisted that he shave it, but Newton resisted. Newton's father felt that his resistance was in direct conflict with the rules and established order of the household. His father continued to ask him to shave the beard and he continued to refuse, causing his father to get physical. This struggle ended with Newton's father striking him and Newton grabbing his father. Newton left his parents' house because his needs to be free were more important than the cohesive environment that the family offered.

This moment was pivotal for Newton because he was now free to come into contact with the individuals who would begin to mold his personal philosophy and idea of consciousness. For example, his first roommate was a young man named Richard Thorne, whose philosophy of love would shape Newton's philosophy concerning women and relationships. Thorne espoused a theory of non-possessive love, which purported that traditional relationships were built on ownership and enslavement of the partner, whereas non-possessive love was based on shared experiences and friendship. Newton compared it with the love we have for our bodies. Individuals have love for their bodies, according to Newton, but did not want to enslave their bodies.

Another personal contact with individuals who would play a large part in shaping Newton's later philosophy was with Donald Warden. While he was involved with Phi Beta Sigma, a social fraternity Newton joined, he would become angry with the sense of oppression he felt. His fraternity brothers suggested that he meet Warden because of the latter's philosophy concerning blackness. Warden ran an organization on the campus of the University of California at Berkeley called the Afro-American Association. The organization's main purpose was to instill pride among blacks stemming from their heritage, history, and contributions to culture and society. Warden was a young lawyer, and he conducted the meetings in the style of a book club. However, because Newton disagreed with Warden's economic philosophy, he began to explore a more cooperative socialistic philosophy as the most beneficial economic strategy for the black community.

JAILED FOR STABBING

While connected to the Afro-American Association, Newton was willing to engage and teach anyone on the subject of his new found socialistic philosophy. Many times, this teaching would take the form of a simple rap session at parties and gatherings among friends and associates. At one such party he attended with his older brother Melvin, he became involved in a discussion with Odell Lee. Newton did not know Lee, but the discussion became violent after Lee associated Newton's rhetoric with that of the Afro-American Association. Lee grabbed Newton because the latter turned his back; in defensive retaliation, Newton stabbed Lee and was later charged with assault with a deadly weapon. Newton pleaded not guilty and went to court against the charges. He was found guilty (according to Newton) because he was adjudicated by a jury not of his peers.[13]

Newton was sentenced to serve time in Alameda County Jail in Oakland in 1964. He would later describe the experience of being incarcerated as being transformative. He was twenty-two when he arrived to serve his sentence. While he was inside, he was involved in a prison uprising, which led to his being placed in solitary confinement, a cell nicknamed the Soul-Breaker. His resolve to face later imprisonments was developed during this period. Newton utilized Gandhi's technique of semi-starvation while incarcerated, so that he would not defecate or urinate during his time in the Soul-Breaker. Newton felt that he was in a battle for control of a portion of his consciousness. By the time that he was released from this sentence, he was able to use his conscious will to tolerate the jail sentences he incurred from activities associated with his Black Panther connections. It was during this time period that his mind became strong enough to feel free in virtually any set of circumstances.

BOBBY SEALE AND THE BLACK PANTHER PARTY

Newton's third experiential moment was when he was introduced to Bobby Seale by Richard Thorne in the spring of 1962. This meeting, because of the events that it precipitated, may have been the most important meeting in life for both Newton and Bobby Seale. From this meeting, Newton was able to develop in Seale a relationship based on common goals and a developing common consciousness. The two seemed to meet at a moment in each others' lives that was conducive for active energy to emanate from their words. It suffices to say that they did not desire to merely talk about what the world should be like.

The premise that the Black Panther Party should not only be a theory-generating organization but should also be actively engaged in revolution was based on the perceived needs of the times and were ideas found in the writings by the philosophers of revolution that Newton studied since beginning college. Much of this philosophy that grounded the thinking of Newton and the other Panthers was built on the writings of Frantz Fanon, Mao Tse Tung, and Che Guevara. At the beginning of this relationship, Newton was incarcerated for the assault of Odell Lee. On his release from jail, Newton rekindled his friendship with Seale and the two began to discuss theory with the expressed purpose of designing a plan of action for the advancement of the black community. In the aftermath of the Watts riots, the Black Panther Party was born. Newton and Seale sat down in the poverty program office of which they were a part and created the Ten Point Platform on October 15, 1966.[14] It was written in the format of wants and beliefs. This format is very similar to that which was used by Franz Fanon, a favorite author of Newton, when he wrote,

> I, the man of color want only, want only this: That the tool never possess the man. That the enslavement of man by man cease forever. That is, of one by another. That it be possible for me to discover and to love man, wherever he may be.[15]

According to Newton, it was from the needs of the people that organization ought to be developed for the lower class. Accordingly, Panthers were born in direct response to the rising consciousness of black people.[16]

For example, based on his readings, Newton realized that the common thread that connected the writings of Mao, Guevara, and Fanon to activities he saw taking place in the black community was that the freedom and dignity of the people were taken from them through the agency of a power elite backed by the threat of deadly force. He concluded along with these writers that it was not pragmatic to use words to battle guns. A favorite phrase of Newton's taken from the writings of Fanon was the "year of the boomerang," meaning that the violence nations inflict on their people finds its way back. However, the use of force to meet force was not the only idea Newton embraced from his readings. It is remembered mainly because it was still a radical idea that blacks should defend their communities, although he was by no means the first to espouse this concept. However, Newton was probably more phenomenal in his teaching of political theory to support an ideology of revolution, and in his belief in the necessity of lifting the consciousness of the black community to spur the freedom movement.

As stated previously, Newton believed and taught that political theory should support the Black Panther ideology of revolution. This is evident in an article written by Newton for the Black Panther newspaper on July 20, 1967. In this short article, Newton announced that "the main function of the party is to awaken the people, teach them the strategic method of resisting a power structure . . ., and to always exemplify revolutionary defiance."[17] According to Newton, to have a means with which to mobilize, the people must be aware of the tools and methods available. The Black Panthers accomplished this with Newton's guidance by remaining prominent as the vanguard of the movement, because Newton believed underground movements are ineffective and out of touch with the people. The Panthers also taught that the people do not invent nor do they initiate revolution; rather, revolution is a consequence of the antecedent behavior of the oppressors' harsh treatment of the people.

Another important part of Huey Newton's political theory is his use of the phrase "the people" as a description of the voiceless underclass as opposed to the way it was used through implication by the constitution framers to include primarily the land holding, white male, political elite.[18] Newton's use of this phrase served two purposes in the teaching of his political theory. It first lifted the consciousness of the people by acknowledging that inherent in the democratic ideal was the innate power of the people to control their own destinies. Second, it served as a declaration of the Panthers' political ideology, which asserted that hegemonic power structures should be abolished in favor of a more egalitarian socialistic power structure such as his concept of intercommunalism.

In Newton's autobiography, chapter 22 is titled "Raising Consciousness."[19] In the prolegomenon to the chapter, Newton defines the Swahili term "nommo" as the power of the word. This is fitting for the discussion that ensues concerning the methods used to raise the consciousness of the people. From the beginning, language is described as the main tool of the Panthers for raising consciousness. It was the goal of the Panthers to change the perception of the people concerning key concepts based on how they were used linguistically. For example, the term "black" was historically used in a negative sense and gained the power to cause self-hatred by its identification with an ethnicity. As neither the majority nor ruling class was black, many who were black desired to distance themselves from this classification. Facing the impossibility of creating such a distance, a nihilistic, self-destructive outlook became a visible part of the contemporary culture. However, by fostering a network of positive connotations surrounding the term black, the Panthers along with others were to force a major re-conceptualization. The same phenomenon can be observed in the usage of the slang term "pig" to represent the police. Newton referred to this process as psychological warfare. By associating an animal with stereotypically undesirable characteristics with police, the Panthers were able to cause a shift in the consciousness of the black community. They could now see that the police force was basically an extension of the long arm of oppression that had been felt for so many years in the black community. Noam Chomsky, when asked about the necessity for slogans and action in reference to the student movement out of which the Panthers were formed, commented that "Without a revolutionary theory or a revolutionary consciousness there is not going be a revolution."[20] Both of these were the primary methods Newton used to raise consciousness.

KNOWLEDGE

Huey P. Newton remains one of the most under-recognized and under-studied thinkers of the civil rights era. Newton pondered a variety of subjects from political philosophy to psychobiology. He wrote some fourteen essays and books, ending with his dissertation titled "War against the Panthers," written while a student at the University of Santa Cruz in 1980. It was not Newton's goal to develop a system, but he did have a desire to use his abilities to understand and alleviate the problem of human oppression beginning with the oppression of his own people. Newton saw himself as akin to the prophets of the Judeo-Christian writings of faith. His autobiography began with a poem intended to be self-defining. It is as follows:

By having no family

I inherited the family of humanity

By having no possessions

I have possessed all.

By rejecting the love of one,

I received the love of all.

By surrendering my life to revolution,

I found eternal life.

Revolutionary Suicide.[21]

It can be seen through this poem that Newton believed his life was serving a high, altruistic purpose to humanity. Whether or not he believed his purpose was fulfilled at his death is secondary to the great energy expended attempting to fulfill this purpose.

Although Newton's writings cover a plethora of subjects, there does appear to be a common thread in their focus. This common thread is summarized in this 1971 statement:

> The original vision of the Black Panther Party was to serve the needs of the oppressed people in our communities and defend them against their oppressors. When the party was initiated we knew that these goals would raise the consciousness of the people and motivate them to move more firmly for their total liberation.[22]

This vision is what drove Newton, the fact of which will be clearly shown throughout the writings to elucidate his understanding of the concept of consciousness and his use of the concept throughout his writings.

The first writing to be analyzed, *The Genius of Huey P. Newton*, was published in 1970. The Panthers were founded in October of 1966.[23] It was at this time that Newton, along with Bobby Seale, penned the ten-point program that was to be the basis of the party's ideology. It was Newton's role to develop new ideas and theories that the party would place into action. Initially, many of Newton's writings were filled with the rhetoric of the revolutionary philosophies of the day. Many of these philosophies had very little relevance to the existential conditions in which Newton and inner city young blacks found themselves during the late 1960s. These philosophies were also disconnected from the dynamics of the particular racial tensions between African Americans and whites during this period. This caused Newton to come to the realization that although these philosophies could serve as a basis for shaping ideas, their relevance was tangential at best. Within this writing, Huey shows glimpses of his subsequent development, such as the nature of his ability to use written prose to express the political theories that shaped the Black Panther organization into a group wielding international influence.

In this collection of writings, which includes letters and essays, Newton begins with a letter addressing a previous communication from Robert Williams of the New Republic of Africa. In the letter, Newton revealed some of the direction that he felt the Panthers should take based on their ideology. The subject matter of the letter is centered on the difference in philosophy of the two organizations. Newton's claim for the difference in the organizational plan of action has little to do with the difference in philosophies and more to do with the theories that supported each organization's analysis of history. The Republic of New Africa was steeped in idealism, while the Panthers read history through the lens of dialectical materialism. It was idealism that caused the Republic of New Africa to consider their present time to be optimal for the building of a nation using the southern states Louisiana, Mississippi, Alabama, Georgia, and South Carolina. In contrast, Newton and the Panthers saw the time period as not yet ready, based on the economic conditions of black people, the lack of military might, and the ability of the United States to colonize "Third World Countries" of that time through the use of advanced technology.

There are several other essays/letters in the book that are of interest, but two in particular demonstrate Newton's focus on raising consciousness as a means of building community and causing social transformation. In the first of these, "Functional Definition of Politics," Newton does not mention consciousness explicitly; however, it is the goal of the article to illumine the true meaning of politics, from which the black community would become conscious of what would be necessary for true social transformation through political means. Newton quickly moves from defining politics to explaining the failed state of black politics as a result of the lack of power found in the black community. Newton builds this discussion on the philosophy of existentialism in the writings of Jean Paul Sartre, through which he describes the black political representative as being absurd (in the Sartreian sense of the word) as such a representative represents no political power. This is because, for Newton, "politics is war without bloodshed"[24] or, in other words, the acquisition of power through political means. Political acts are always backed by the threat of a consequence from the community that elects the representative, except in the case of the black representative, who is sent from a community that has no power because it lacks the means to acquire power. These means would include, for example, major land holdings, businesses that are essential to the fulfillment of the American way of life (i.e., General Motors), or organized military might.

In the next essay, "Message from the Minister of Defense: Huey P. Newton on the Peace Movement," Newton continues the line of thought by examining the phenomenon of the black self. This essay deals with consciousness explicitly by first focusing on the subconscious and the role it plays in determining human perspective. Newton refers to the work of Sigmund Freud and Karl Marx as he communicates his position concerning the subconscious. For Newton, the epitome of being human is to be free. Accordingly, Newton lists two major factors that have a determining effect on the human individual, specifically the black self, to actualize freedom. This idea of freedom can be said to have its beginnings in the concept of "Free Will." From this concept grows the desire to have a certain type of existence. Newton seems to imply that freedom is connected to the idea of having many choices as opposed to a very limited number of choices determined by outside influences targeting the subconscious. To gain freedom from this deterministic pattern of life, the individual has to become conscious of the internal forces that create appetites and aversions that display themselves through various behaviors.

Newton's reading of Marx focuses on the external forces that determine behavior. Marx targeted the mode of production when he contemplated what would be necessary to constitute freedom—namely, a transition from a forced mode of production to a creative mode of production. In the forced mode of production, individuals seek to earn a living through their production and are in effect forced to produce non-creatively because those who have the capital to purchase this production become the owners of the production and its producer. These owners determine what is produced, what is purchased, and in essence who lives or dies. Newton, as well as Marx, believed that in order for individuals to break free of this type of passive slavery, the system of private ownership would have to be destroyed.

The purpose for Newton's use of consciousness in this collection of essays is first to instruct. It was Newton's belief that his theories were correct, but they required such a paradigm shift that they would have to be continuously taught and demonstrated to the black community. This was because both internal and external factors had made the black community mentally and physically complicit in their own subaltern status. Newton attributed this phenomenon to a lack of knowledge on the part of blacks concerning their individual and social existence. Next, Newton believed that this style of writing would arouse emotion in any area of high black population, inclining them to bind closer and form a real community based not just on physical similarities but also consciousness, and also this new community would search for solutions that would lead to social transformation.

Huey Newton was quickly becoming a person recognized nationally and internationally for his radical thoughts concerning the process of revolution, community development, and social transformation. These factors led Newton to make several public appearances to garner support for the Panther philosophy and also to serve as fundraising opportunities. Yale was picked as the location to make one of these appearances because of its proximity to New York, the site where many Panthers were standing trial. Erik Erikson was included in this forum that Newton planned, which took place in 1971. Erikson and others associated with the forum thought it good if Newton and he discussed certain issues for the purpose of finding common bases from which to understand Newton's point of view. Newton took this opportunity to expose the Yale student body to the Black Panthers and their leaders, and to also educate the student body on the nature of the oppressive forces that led to the creation of the Panthers.

In this work, *In Search of Common Ground*, several issues concerning the Panther ideology were philosophically addressed in a manner that the crowd was not expecting to hear from a radical such as Newton.[25] The first of these issues to receive philosophical treatment was which type of socioeconomic structure would best benefit the communities that the Panthers saw as being oppressed. Newton's philosophical argument for intercommunalism, his proposed socioeconomic structure, takes the form of a historical discussion of Panther ideology based on the philosophies that grounded them. Newton's first premise comes from the Marxist notion of flux, which posits that everything is in a state of constant change. For Newton, this can only be true if the world is a material world. This claim is taken as an a priori fact, and on the basis of this, he also held that the positivist principle that humans would eventually be able to solve all problems facing humanity was true. From this basic grounding, he defines consciousness as the ability to observe, analyze, and respond to the material world.

Another basic premise on which Newton builds his philosophy is the fundamental internal contradiction of all things. For him, this premise is antithetical to the Western mindset. The example he gives to prove this comes from religion. According to him, African Gods south of the Sahara were pairs, representing evil and good. His claim was that all peoples create their Gods in their own image, based on their understanding of the world in which they live.[26] For him, this necessarily meant that the Africans saw humans as being a combination of both good and evil. By comparison, the Western concept of God is divided, with good being upward in Heaven and evil being downward in Hell. This meant, accordingly, that in the Western mindset, people were either good or bad. Newton also felt that this basic understanding of the internal makeup of the human mind had implications for social interactions among classes and communities. This premise led to another inherent condition of struggle, which can be defined as the attempt or the intense desire to change.

These premises formed the ideological origins of the Panthers. When the Panthers began, based on the contradictions of their experience, they thought it necessary to desire a place or nation to call home. Their ideology was consequently nationalistic. However, after studying history more closely, they realized that the period of newly created nations had at last come to a slowdown. Most inhabitable lands globally were now inhabited. If black people were to create a nation, the development of military might or some other powerful agent would be needed for this great undertaking. The lack of viability in this course of action caused the Panthers to recognize its inherent contradiction. From this ideological locale and through realizing inherent contradictions in their ideologies, the Panthers went through three more ideological shifts. These shifts were from nationalists to revolutionary nationalists, from revolutionary nationalists to internationalists, and from internationalists to intercommunalists, all of which were brought about by intense contradictions found in their everyday lived experience.

Revolutionary nationalists differ from nationalists in that they want radical change in the nation in which they already live. This change is also described as being a complete change in the economic system, social relationships, and political processes. This type of nationalistic ideology carried with it the necessity of great numbers of supporters. Realizing this, the Panthers began to consider blacks outside the continent of Africa as a dispersed colony. This in turn brought out another contradiction in the logic being used. To generate sufficient force to overcome the force of oppression, alignment with other oppressed peoples, regardless of their ethnicity, was thought to be the way. To express this new found solidarity with other peoples around the world, the term nationalist was replaced by internationalist. This gave to their philosophy a wider scope of activity and influence throughout the world. However, there was still a contradiction in this new ideology, because if the goal was to form a nation, then there were still certain agents at work that would cause this goal to be elusive at best. As technology had conferred the ability to communicate over long distances and the same was true for travel, these two factors made it easier for the more powerful nation to control the less powerful nations. This made it difficult to think of the less powerful nations as independent, sovereign nation-states. His observation of these conditions led Newton to borrow Marshall McLuhan's term "global village" in his acknowledgement that "the communication revolution, combined with the expansive domination of the American empire, has created the global village."

From this conclusion, the concept that the less powerful nations were no more than communities was identified. Community was defined as "a small unit with a comprehensive collection of institutions that exist to serve a small group of people." In keeping with this logic, it was reasoned that the oppression faced in nations such as Vietnam was the same as that faced in Oakland, differing only in degree. With this in mind, the Panthers made their third and final shift in logic to intercommunalism: "The struggle in the world today is between the small circle that administers and profits from the empire of the United States and the peoples of the world who want to determine their own destinies."[27]

Consciousness is defined early in the work and then used to explicate the human being's ability to understand and change the phenomenological existence experienced. There is also at work an assumption that if the experience is different, then it stands to reason that the consciousness is different, thus creating different cultures and different groups. Newton restates in this text that the primary concern of the Black Panther Party is to lift the consciousness of the people through theory and action to the point where they see exactly what is controlling them and what is oppressing them, and therefore see exactly what has to be done. This is a reference to the earlier work, which speaks of internal and external factors that affect the individual's ability to be free.[28] The point is also made that collective consciousness is possible and is necessary for true human community to exist, although Newton does not elaborate.

The usage of the word "consciousness" and its definition is explicit. It is in these conversations that Newton makes a deliberate effort to outline the philosophical basis for the political theory that drives the active participation of the organization in the struggle to rid blacks of oppressive forces. In doing so, Newton defines consciousness and also describes in detail the placement of the concept within the framework of intercommunalism. As stated earlier, he defines himself as a Marxist theorist who posits that all substance is material and exists in a state of flux. He admits that his premises are based on a priori assumptions and does not attempt to explain concepts such as what are thoughts. Are thoughts physically constructed? If so, might they somehow be physically extracted from one individual and placed in another? For Newton, such questions are unnecessary to his overall purpose, which is to show that consciousness can be increased or raised by providing more sensory experience. When consciousness is raised, the individual is changed.

The major manifestation of that change as Newton saw it was the energy derived from the changed consciousness, because he believed it caused movement leading to transformation on a substantive level.

Newton's purpose for the use of consciousness as a framework was to demonstrate to the Yale student body and the American public at large the significance of an environment in which one group was allowed to oppress another. The result of a lived experience in such an environment is the development of a type of knowledge that leads to a new consciousness. This new consciousness, as stated previously, would eventually lead toward transformation. Newton was also aware that within this forum, his words would have a similar effect of causing a shift in consciousness that, he believed, could eventually lead to a renewed spirit of human brotherhood. On this matter Newton states,

> No, I think that whether we like it or not, dialectics would make it necessary to have a universal identity. If we do not have a universal identity, then we will have cultural, racial, and religious chauvinism, the kind of ethnocentrism we have now.[29]

In 1972, a compilation of letters and speeches of Newton was published in order that the party's insiders and sympathizers could have a clear sense of direction concerning party ideas, stances on important issues, and future goals. This compilation was titled *To Die for the People*, and through its historical layout of writings, it presents the growth and the framework through which the Panthers formed their views.[30] Essentially, it continues where *The Search for Common Ground* convenes by demonstrating the practice of community development and social transformation. Some of the proclamations and letters have been reprinted in this work to demonstrate the continuity and growth in thought. There are new concepts that are worth notice, two of which will be discussed here in some detail. They are titled "On the Relevance of the Church" and "He Won't Bleed Me."

In "On the Relevance of the Church," Newton describes in detail the failures of the Panthers to maintain proper community ties because of a misunderstanding of the nature and the effect of separating the organization from the church. As mentioned earlier, the Panthers' ideology was built on a premise that the world is a material world. This premise would put the Panthers in direct conflict with most churches,

whose essential theological premise was that God is a spirit. Many of
the Panthers, including Newton, believed that the church was directing the people toward incorrect goals because of illogical conclusions
formed from their misconceived theological premise. This difference
caused the Panthers to publicly dismiss the church as an ineffective
institution. The problem with this action is that it did not take into consideration the history of the church in the total black experience. Also,
Newton discounted the wordplay embedded in the church's theological language, which contained many goals and practices found in the
Panther philosophy. The only difference is that in the church, they were
stated using metaphor. On realizing this error, Newton interjected his
quasi-philosophy of religion by putting forth the nature of God based
on a materialist view of the world. Newton described God as being
equal to human ignorance. As knowledge increases, the need for the
human subconscious creation of God subsides. Newton's compared the
Panther's leave from the church to the moment an individual feels his
or need for God subside.

In "He Won't Bleed Me," Newton shows the connection between the
attempt to raise the consciousness of the people and the creative arts.
This work analyzes a movie created by Melvin Van Peebles in which
the main character, Sweetback, is used to demonstrate the experience
of the black individual of sub-community coming to consciousness
by realizing that a true community means unity, which leads in turn
to transformation. Newton calls his analysis a revolutionary analysis
because he views the movie through the lens of its ability to demonstrate
revolutionary change on multiple levels. The overarching message of
this movie is that from knowledge comes unity and from unity comes
transformation. This is shown in the following quote where Newton
speaks of the community in the process of becoming transformed by
consciousness from an oppressed community to a liberated one:

> For a long time the black community has been a collection of
> people who survive together in one place, but unity is essential for
> liberation as well as survival. When there is unity, the faith of one
> becomes the faith of another, as in the case of Sweetback and Moo
> Moo. When we have our consciousness increased, victimizers will
> always try to prevent this unity. And we must understand that the
> victimizers will always try to prevent this unity.[31]

The overall compilation *To Die for the People* demonstrated the continuity of thought in Newton's theories, and his belief in the necessity of raising consciousness through increased knowledge. This increase of knowledge that in turn increased consciousness was, for him, the first step in revolution. He believed that multiple instructional techniques could be used to increase consciousness. The lectures, the movie analysis, the letters, and even the title were all different methods that he felt necessary to the raising of consciousness. The book in total, for him, is a component of the first step of the revolution.

Revolutionary Suicide was not only the title of Newton's 1973 autobiography but also the name for the philosophical approach, which Newton utilized to explain how an individual who was truly committed to the movement should give of himself.[32] Besides its biographical material, this work is very important because it outlines many of the premises and philosophical conclusions on which the actions of the Panther organization were built. Newton begins the work by offering his life as typical of black life, especially that of the underclass of black life. First, he describes life in the South. Next, he writes about the family's migration to Oakland. From there, Newton narrates the story of his years in school interlaced with the story of hanging out with his friends later to become what he terms the "Brothers on the Block." These personal themes are used to demonstrate the general nature of black life. Moreover, Newton constantly puts forth the idea that through all of the poverty, blacks continued to have a way of doing things, a culture, and an aesthetic. The culture can be glimpsed in the way Newton describes his early training from his brother. Newton states, "In our family there was a tradition that each had a responsibility for a younger one, looking after him at play, feeding him, taking him to school. This was called giving the newborn to an older brother or sister."[33] Of the aesthetic, Newton writes,

> Often, when others expect to find me depressed by difficult circumstances, and especially by the extreme condition of prison, they see that I look at things in another way. Not that I am happy with the suffering; I simply refuse to be defeated by it.[34]

Two chapters of Newton's autobiography are especially relevant to this research. The first of these is titled "Raising Consciousness." In this chapter, Newton discusses the effect his reading of Nietzsche had on his philosophical insights. He is clear that Nietzsche had a large influence on the development of his and the entire Panther organization's philosophy. The greatest part of this influence came in the way Nietzsche described phenomena. In short, Nietzsche argues that man describes phenomena as good or evil depending on the way it benefits the descriptor and the descriptor's group. This is done, according to Nietzsche, to satisfy the will to power that lies within each person. Newton used this method of phenomenology to raise the consciousness of the people, as seen in the shift of meaning in the usage of the word black. According to Newton, the word was connected to negative linguistic characterizations that caused black people to have an inferiority complex. As blacks became aware of this negative characteristic, they began to use the word in a more positive manner. The new usage of the word black prompted more positive displays of a lifted self-image.

Newton also describes Nietzsche's comparison of this methodology with the manner in which Christians dealt with the derogatory portrayal of the Christian church by the Roman Empire. Newton accepts Nietzsche's explanation that the consciousness of people was raised through this phenomenon. He felt that the biggest tool of the ruling circle was the threat of physical harm the community felt. It became important that the community understand that the threat of physical harm was not remote, but immediate and enforced by the neighborhood police department. Newton realized that the image of the police department as the keeper of peace had to be changed in order for the black community to see the threat of physical harm represented by the police. Therefore, the effect of calling the police pigs was twofold. It caused the black community to realize that the police served the purpose of providing a physical front for the establishment. Moreover, it caused many whites to reexamine themselves and, after doing so, to experience feelings of guilt and shame. Finally, Newton also uses this phenomenology to address metaphysical concerns through the slogan "All Power to the People." Simply put, this term was used to demonstrate the nature of Newton's philosophy of religion. He felt that outside of man there was no God and that humans should not relinquish their power to change the world to a powerless conception of divinity.

In the last chapter of the book, Newton describes his concept of revolutionary suicide. In this short epilogue, he explains the concept on the basis of which the entire book is named and the concept by which he lived. He begins by making an analogy using an African saying, "I Am We." This is done to make the point that his life and that of his friends were hopelessly doomed as an ancillary result of the oppressive environment in which they lived. The deterministic paths they would choose led them to death, jail, or insanity. However, even as the people's level of understanding of the reason for their limitations varied, so did their fear of the threat of death and also the commitment to the possibility of transformation. If a person is driven by life to some terrible end, without intentionally desiring this result, then this is reactionary suicide. However, if the person realizes his plight and dedicates his life to the possibility of transformation, regardless of how futile the effort, then he has engaged in revolutionary suicide. To be a revolutionary, according to Newton, an individual necessarily assumes that he or she is knowledgeable of the causes of his or her situation and is an active participant in his or her change. Revolutionary suicide is a philosophy that has as much to do with a person's perception of existence as it has to do with the manner in which the individual engages social and political change.

This work in its entirety depicts Newton's coming to consciousness and his active social and political transformation. Early in the book, Newton is faced with choices of what type of individual he will become and also how he will view life. These choices were paramount because they would also determine how he would conceive future ideas. Once he made his choice to become a revolutionary, his goals and actions would always reflect the evolution of his consciousness as he gave himself totally to the realization of his desired experience. The book demonstrates this process as he goes from youth in his parents' home to become a man dedicated to the creation of free community based on an assumption that this type of community is possible and necessary in order for blacks to actualize their fullest potential. For Newton, the fullest potential is realized through historical knowledge of the conditions of one's own communal existence and also through the acquisition of power giving the community the ability to maintain its freedom.

The work is very explicit about consciousness because Newton's objective is to cause readers to reflect on their own existence, whether it be reactionary or revolutionary, and also to bring to the fore the struggles that the desire to be free could possibly mandate. He creates this type of pedagogical approach through the narration of his biography while exploring the type of choice he made to be free, which he called "Revolutionary Suicide."[35] Newton writes, "Life does not always begin at birth. My life was forged in the lives of my parents before I was born, and even earlier in the history of all black people. It is all of a piece."[36] Because revolutionary suicide is an individual choice, it seems that the book aimed at the creation of a certain type of community, by causing individuals to make the conscious choice of being revolutionary as opposed to being reactionary. Newton admits his owns struggle in making this choice by saying,

> I saw all my turmoil in terms of racism and exploitation and the obvious discrepancies between the have and the have-nots. I was trying to figure out how to avoid being crushed and losing respect for myself, how to keep from embracing the oppressor that had already maimed my family and community.[37]

Newton accomplishes his task by celebrating his own choices while also embracing the consequences they caused—for example, his jail sentence: "Jail is an odd place to find freedom. I first found mine in the Alameda County Jail in Oakland in 1964."[38] He also marries his story to the coming of consciousness of the black community. In a very real way, he is saying the individual choice has to be made to transform the community or the community will cease to exist. He writes,

> I do not think that life will change for the better without an assault on the Establishment, which goes on exploiting the wretched of the earth. This belief lies at the heart of the concept of revolutionary suicide. This it is better to oppose the forces that would drive me to self-murder than to endure them. Although I risk the possibility of death, there is at least the possibility, if not the probability, of changing intolerable conditions.[39]

In 1974, Newton wrote a paper titled "The Mind is Flesh" in which very dense academic language is used to drive home the point that as the environment changes, so does the human body and so also the mind, because according to Newton, the mind is flesh. This paper begins by giving a short historical account of the argument concerning the mind–body problem, which reached its zenith with the philosophy of Descartes. Of this, Newton writes his counter argument using the theorem put forth by Søren Kierkegaard, which states, "the mind is flesh."[40] To this point, Newton adds that the major concept that necessarily follows this theorem is that the mind, which is flesh and is inseparable from the body, has its existence in the same location as the body. That location is the physical environment. The introduction concludes with the main focus of the paper, which is "to change the environment is to change the mind at the phenomenal level."[41]

After the introduction of the paper, Newton takes to task the traditional understanding of the Cartesian mind–body argument, which posits that there are two types of substances existing in the universe. These two substances are matter and mind (spirit). Matter can be known through the senses and exists in time and space. Accordingly, mind cannot be known in this manner and can only be known by the individual and exists outside of time and space. From these premises, many extrapolated that the human body contained both these substances, and at the death of the body, the mind was able to escape its physical prison while continuing to function and to exist. The major part of this argument that Newton is concerned with, however, is the conclusion drawn from these premises, which allows for the creation of two spheres of existence for the individual, one sphere being physical and external, and the other being spiritual and internal. Newton focuses on the conflict that arises out of this argument to form his greater conclusion. First, nothing can be said to exist internally if it does not exist in time and space, for not existing in time and space means that there is no physical location, internal or external. The second begs the question of how a stimulus with a physical source can generate a mental response or vice versa.

Newton uses these two points as the impetus for the remainder of the paper. His goal is to elucidate the institution of physical controls through so-called mind control. Newton puts forth the concept that anything created for the purpose of influencing or controlling the mind also does the same to the body. For Newton, there is no separation between the mind and the body; they both exist in the material world. This argument is based on Newton's understanding of the dialectical–materialist framework, which basically states that everything that exists has its existence in the material world. Newton furthers his argument by indirectly making the point that everything that exists in the material world is interconnected, thereby accounting for the environmental changes affecting the evolution of humanity and humanity's effect on the environment. This makes space for the notion that the private life as understood under the Cartesian argument is at best a misnomer, because, in a totally material world, there is always the possibility of knowing individuals internally and of being controlled internally.

Next, Newton lists several examples of efforts by individuals and organizations to develop items and processes aimed at controlling or modifying behavior. The summary point and purpose of this listing is to speak of their function in causing the separation of the "I" from the "It." This is the process of alienation where the mind is caused to believe that it exists over and against the body. When this process is successful, according to Newton, the person becomes enslaved to an idea of existence separate from the physical body. Of this Newton states,

> It is, then, the task of dialectical materialism to invoke the entire human body in a complete social-historical context whenever the concepts "mind" or "brain" are brought to play in the dialogue of alienation that modern science has become. Our field is real life where each arbitrary order of abstraction (mind-brain-body) is always a function of human flesh and blood. And the sum of these abstractions is the soul. And that the soul and the ego may be congruous when the ego (the "I") and the race are perceived as functions of each other always and everywhere. Thus, dialectical materialism presses, always, toward a structuralism of dynamic process.[42]

In other words, for Newton, the dialectical materialist must make perfectly clear, in any conversation concerning actions aimed at limiting or restricting the mind, that limitations on the mind are limitations on the body. When this is done, he believed people would be more conscious of those processes and items that have been created to enslave and to oppress.

It is unclear whether or not Newton intended to have the work published, or was only working out his philosophy. However, his paper does have implications for community development. He attempts to explicitly outline the result of both raising and not raising the consciousness of the community concerning the mind–body problem. For him, when it is done, the community will be able to live free, but when it is not done, the community will be enslaved.

War against the Panthers is the title of Newton's little-known dissertation, which he completed in 1980 at the University of California, Santa Cruz. In this work, Newton creates a construct from which to view American reaction to dissent. The basic argument in the dissertation is that American society was based on a racially biased social philosophy, and to maintain that philosophy, the new government kept large portions of the population disenfranchised. For this reason, he states that from the beginning of the American Republic, those in power have used their power to maintain their social and economic advantage.

Furthermore, their repressive techniques have included agencies of disinformation, undercover agents, provocateurs, harassment, and informants, all of which were used to eradicate the voice of dissent. Moreover, the targets of these actions from the government were chosen for their otherness in race, religion, and political ideology. The Panthers were also included in the list of organizations being repressed. After listing several historical incidents, Newton began to focus solely on the repression experienced by the Panther Party. In writing in this fashion, he is able to demonstrate that the activity of the Panthers was not the only reason for the repression they suffered. He accomplishes this task by giving the history of the party, the ideology, and the major activities in which the Panthers engaged. Much of this information was given in the previously discussed writings of Newton; however, revolutionary intercommunalism is mentioned as a socialist ideology aimed at "meet[ing] the daily needs of the people by developing positive institutions within their communities and to organize the communities politically around these programs."[43]

This work is demonstrative of the types of writing Newton engaged in after completing his bachelor's degree in 1974. These writings exhibit the highly analytical style Newton adopted from the philosophies he digested through the years. For him, it was now important to analyze and document the reaction of opposing forces to the revolutionary activity of the Panthers and others so that future activists would be fully aware of the high cost of their actions. Moreover, to avoid confusion, Newton places the revolutionary strivings of the Panthers in their proper context among others whose historical demonstrations of dissent brought an equal reaction from those who sought to repress. In essence, the dissertation was focused on raising the consciousness of future revolutionary leaders and activists. It also had as a purpose the sharing of the proper steps in building intercommunal institutions and offered explanations for the failings of the Panthers. By doing so, Newton proved that repression is common to all struggles in America for liberty and equality. Newton then indicates, in a very subtle manner, that it is possible for thoughts and the expression of those thoughts to be forcibly repressed if they have the potential to undermine the status quo for the sake of social transformation and the economic mobility of the underclass.

The last scholarly work of Newton to be mentioned in this section is a very short analytic paper titled the "The Crash of Flight 90," which was co-written with famed biologist, Robert Trivers. The paper consists of brief descriptive and analytical statements following each verbal exchange between the pilot and co-pilot. The purpose of the work was to ascribe some causal action to the crash that occurred in 1982 and both the scholars agreed that causal action to be self-deception. The brevity of this work hinders its analysis in the same manner as the other works; however, its importance to the scope of Newton's interpretation of the idea of consciousness is pivotal. This is because it makes space for an explanation of the resistance many have to the raising of their consciousness. The analysis points out that self-deception requires a lesser effort to envelop the individual being deceived because it becomes a new perspective from which to perceive. It was also stipulated that self-deception developed in humans as a coping mechanism mostly to deal with an unwanted situation. As an inherent trait or quality in humans, it necessarily follows that when any attempt is made to raise the consciousness of a particular community, it will be met with some amount of resistance stemming from possible impending acts of repression or a desire to resist change. In essence, fear of repression hinders raising of consciousness just as actual repression does. Accordingly, fear also causes the individual to be a reactionary, and not a revolutionary, which creates a major obstacle to the raising of consciousness.

NOTES

1 Robert Trivers, *Natural Selection and Social Theory: Selected Papers of Robert L. Trivers* (New York: Oxford University Press, 2002), 259.

2 Ibid.

3 Erikson and Newton, *In Search of Common Ground*, 49 (see chap. 1, n. 16).

4 Ibid.
5 J. L. Jeffries, *Huey P. Newton: The Radical Theorist* (Jackson: University Press of Mississippi, 2002), ix–xiv.
6 A term used by Dr. Robert Franklin in his book, *Liberating Visions*, to describe the fundamental personality of each subject in that work.
7 Thomas A. Spragens, *Understanding Political Theory* (New York: St. Martin's Press, 1976), 1.
8 Erikson and Newton, *In Search of Common Ground*, 14–17 (see chap. 1, n. 16).
9 Matthew W. Hughey, "The Pedagogy of Huey P. Newton: Critical Reflections on Education in His Writings and Speeches," *Journal of Black Studies*, 38, no. 2 (2007): 209–31, accessed April 11, 2012, http://jbs.sagepub.com/content/38/2/209. abstract?cited-by=yes.
10 Newton, *Revolutionary Suicide*, 56 (see chap. 1, n. 22).
11 Hughey, "Pedagogy of Huey P. Newton," http://jbs.sagepub.com/content/38/2/209. abstract?cited-by=yes.
12 Marian Kempny and Aldona Jawłowska, *Identity in Transformation: Postmodernity, Postcommunism, and Globalization* (Westport: Praeger, 2002), 105.
13 Newton, *Revolutionary Suicide*, 106 (see chap. 1, n. 22).
14 Seale, *Seize the Time*, 62 (see chap. 1, n. 17).
15 Frantz Fanon, *Black Skin, White Mask* (New York: Grove Press, 1967), 231.
16 Newton, *Revolutionary Suicide*, 128 (see chap. 1, n. 22).
17 Huey P. Newton, *To Die for the People: The Writings of Huey P. Newton* (New York: Random House, 1972), 15.
18 Charles Austin Beard, *An Economic Interpretation of the Constitution* (New York: Free Press, 1913), 1–19.
19 Newton, *Revolutionary Suicide*, 173 (see chap. 1, n. 22).
20 Noam Chomsky and Carlos Peregrín Otero, *Language and Politics* (Oakland: AK Press, 2004), 109.
21 Newton, *Revolutionary Suicide*, x (see chap. 1, n. 22).
22 Huey P. Newton, David Hilliard, and Donald Weise, *The Huey P. Newton Reader* (New York: Seven Stories Press, 2002), 209.
23 Huey P. Newton, *The Genius of Huey Newton* (Oakland: Awesome Records, 1993), 1–22.
24 Ibid., 18.
25 Erikson and Newton, *In Search of Common Ground*, 14–17 (see chap. 1, n. 16).
26 Ibid., 130.
27 Ibid., 30–31.
28 Ibid.
29 Ibid., 53–54.
30 Newton, *To Die for the People*, xix–xxi.
31 Ibid., 131.
32 Ibid., 13.
33 Newton, *Revolutionary Suicide*, 13 (see chap. 1, n. 22).
34 Ibid.

35 Ibid., 11.
36 Ibid., 11.
37 Ibid., 62.
38 Ibid., 99.
39 Ibid., 5.
40 Newton, Hilliard, and Weise, *Huey P. Newton Reader*, 317.
41 Ibid., 317
42 Ibid., 293.
43 Huey P. Newton, *War against the Panthers: A Study of Repression in America* (New York: Harlem River Press, 1996), 30.

5

THE SEARCH FOR COMMON GROUND

In the preceding chapters, the experiences and the knowledge gained from those experiences were analyzed with the intent of creating a foundation to build a comparison of the ideas of consciousness in Thurman's and Newton's writings. In this chapter, the ideas of consciousness will be compared to determine whether confluence exists in the understanding of consciousness or in the uses of the ideas of consciousness as a forming agent of the philosophies of Thurman and Newton. Special consideration will be given to the uses of consciousness as a catalyst in their construction of a theory for community development and social transformation. As stated previously, it is not the purpose of this study to determine which ideas of consciousness were better. The purpose is to compare the ideas to show the existence of confluence.

THURMAN'S IDEA OF CONSCIOUSNESS

Thurman's idea of consciousness is described in the works chosen for this study in a progressive but non-systematic manner. The works were written with the understanding that in order for the reader to grasp the full breadth of meaning of Thurman's theology, the entire collection would have to be absorbed. The focus of this study is centered on the idea of consciousness that necessarily contributes to need for a definition of Thurman's and Newton's respective idea of consciousness. Thurman's definition of consciousness grows from his philosophical theology in which God as the source of all that exists is taken for granted. Therefore, Thurman seeks first to reveal and describe the overall nature of consciousness. After doing so, Thurman makes a connection to the individual by describing consciousness as inherent quality of being. His description of the mind as the cause and product of consciousness facilitates an understanding of his discussion of the inner spirit.

Thurman's first articulation of a concise definition for consciousness as a phenomenon can be found in "Mysticism and Social Change," which was published in 1939.[1] In this writing, a short explication is given of the connection between his brand of mysticism and social ethics. According to Thurman, the motive of the work was a realization of the lack of knowledge concerning mysticism, for which he quotes Bertrand Russell: "What is clear in all cases and ethically characteristic of mysticism is absence of indignation or protest, acceptance with joy, disbelief in the ultimate truth of the division into two hostile camps, the good and the bad."[2] It is from this point that the conversation concerning the social ethics of mysticism ensues. However, it is in the midst of discussion that Thurman's idea of consciousness comes to light. In fact, it does not appear that Thurman can unravel the meaning behind the usage of the term mysticism without some explanation of the idea of consciousness.

Thurman relies on the narrative format to illuminate the subject of mysticism. He begins by pointing out the basic premise of mysticism, that all life is one. He writes, "All life is one and yet life seems to move in such intimate circles of awful individuality."[3] To fully understand Thurman's dictum, a small explanation from his source is necessary. As we have seen, Thurman was involved in an independent special study with the renowned mystic and scholar, Rufus Jones, and many of his ideas, as well as his methodology, came from this source. However, the foundation of Thurman's understandings of the universe was derived during his youth in Daytona, Florida. Thurman was an avid observer of nature and as such spent large amounts of time meditating and communicating with nature, particularly with a large oak tree in his yard. According to Thurman, even on return visits after leaving home to receive an education, it was the tree that would be included high on the list of purposes for his visits. Thurman wrote in his autobiography, "As for me, on each visit I would go to my oak tree to lean against it for an intense moment of past intimacy."[4] In the tree, he found a focal point and a way to express his belief that all of life was one. Thurman's moments with the tree reaffirmed that through this oneness with all life, a direct connection could be experienced with the Holy.

The fact of this connection for Thurman was communicated in his realization that it is God who becomes being. Thurman discusses this in his explanation of the urge toward community in all individuals. He purports that a characteristic of all life is this urge for the experience of community. For him, it follows necessarily that the basis for this urge is that the

> Mind of God realizes Itself in time, and that there are observable patterns or sequences in creation. From this point of view, all time-space manifestations of substance—in short, all things, even existence itself—are regarded as the Mind of God coming to Itself in time and space.[5]

This phenomenon becomes the source of all consciousness. Each individual being (which represents the totality of beingness) has the urge to rejoin the whole. The whole, for Thurman, is the Holy or the mind of God. This urge (or desired experience) creates consciousness of individuality or self-consciousness. Thurman believed that consciousness is or has the ultimate purpose of reattachment to the whole or the Holy. The individual or separated being, which is now conscious, also realizes the difficulty in maintaining its focus on God due to worldly attachments that Thurman recognized as sin or evil. It is for this reason that the individual becomes committed to transcending or transforming anything that distorts his intended focus. Accordingly, the ability to be conscious is derived from the mind of God. Consciousness, which for Thurman on some level becomes the recognition of the separateness from God and the recognition of different phenomena that distort the view of God, is brought about by the great desire to return to God. Thurman refers to this event as actively reflecting on experience.[6]

Much of the language Thurman uses to substantiate his premises can be found in the writings of other mystic thinkers with which he was acquainted through his readings. In a sermon of Meister Eckhart titled "The Kingdom of God is at Hand," Eckhart states,

> There is an agent in my soul which is perfectly sensitive to God. I am as sure of this as I am that I am alive: nothing is as near to me as God is. God is nearer to me than I am to myself. My being depends on God's intimate presence.[7]

Rufus Jones commented "that the divine and human, God and man, are not wholly sundered."[8] These statements are in direct correlation with Thurman's belief that consciousness begins in God's mind having the desire to return to itself in the form of the life agent in humans realizing the God presence within. For Thurman and others, consciousness is not just divinely created but it is divine. It is literally of God. Accordingly, another writer with whom Thurman came into contact, Ralph Waldo Emerson, wrote,

> We call God a Mind. He has revealed himself as a spirit. But what do we know of mind, but through the unfolding of this principle in our own breasts? That unbounded spiritual energy which we call God, is conceived by us only through consciousness, through the knowledge of ourselves.[9]

For Thurman, it is a simple concept. In the process of God participating in the creation through self-division, certain divine qualities are transmitted to the human creation specifically, one of which is the ability to reflect on the experience of being or, in a word, consciousness.

So then consciousness, as found in Thurman's writings, is an inherent quality of being. In his writings, being was always viewed and described through the lens of blackness. Coming to existence in a moment when racial prejudice affected all of American life, Thurman could hardly escape being transformed by this situational contact. So much so, that when he began to expound on the meaning of being, also discussing the fact that consciousness is an inherent quality of being, his exposition was a consequence of his own blackness.

The study of what it means to be, or more accurately phenomenology, is believed to have started with Franz Brentano. Phenomenological nomenclature was developed by Edmund Husserl and later proponents such as Martin Heidegger. However, the study of being and existence can be found to be a part of philosophy from its ancient beginnings. In the *Metaphysics*, Aristotle wrote, "There is a science which investigates being as being and the attributes which belong to this in virtue of its own nature." In this section of the *Metaphysics*, Aristotle is attempting to describe the parameters of an ontological or phenomenological study. Perspective or frame of reference has also continually determined how these phenomena, specifically as they apply to human existence, are described. For example, Heidegger writes concerning Aristotle's thoughts about a human being's existence in the world, "perception, thinking, wanting are not experiences . . . but instead deal with the being of a human being (or of living beings in general) in the world."[10] In other words, Heidegger is claiming that there are aspects of being that cannot be separated from the study of being when investigating its nature.

According to James Bryant and Paget Henry, in their paper presented at the 2006 Thurman Roundtable at Temple University, "Thurman's phenomenology begins with descriptive elaborations of his phenomenal re-presentation to consciousness of the racialized social reality of segregated America."[11] This is important because of Thurman's description of consciousness as an inherent quality of being. Given that the existence of consciousness necessarily refers to the active usage of the term, that is, consciousness of some particular phenomenon, Thurman always, when describing his own existence, began from the perspective of his knowledge of the world through the eyes of the black experience. In the prologue to one of Thurman's earliest works, *Deep River*, he wrote,

> In what is written here there is at work the movement of the creative spirit of God as it has sought under great odds to tutor my rebellious spirit in conflict with some of the tragedies of my social experience.[12]

Later in the same work, Thurman outlines in detail his understanding of the connection between perspective and the shaping of ideas through experience. As for Thurman consciousness cannot be separated from human existence, it also follows that subjectivity or perspective cannot be separated. He writes that "the amazing transformation of the material ideals, concepts, and ideologies of a whole nation in one generation is a case in point. It is the nature of life that we are kneaded and molded by our experience of life."[13] His comments appear congruent with other major thinkers of his day on the subject of the relationship between consciousness, being, and perspective.

In the writings of Thurman, the mind of God engages in the development and activity of consciousness in an intimate way. The framework from which to understand this concept begins with the solitary life of the individual mystic who desires the experience of community. This desire brings about an awareness of the presence of community wherever it is found in nature. Thurman writes, "The life of the mystic is worked out in the life of men and things. There is an element of the solitariness in his experience."[14] From this mystic framework, he is able to build an understanding of how it can be said that mind is both product and cause of consciousness. As stated earlier, the mystic understands all life as being one. The mystic concludes that even within an experience of extreme solitude, there is no question about the existence of being itself. This is very different from the Cartesian "dubito ergo cogito ergo sum" (I doubt, therefore I think, therefore I am). There is simply the descriptive affirmation that being is, and that through this experience of being, the mystic realizes himself as deeply interconnected with being. In this experience of oneness with being, the mystic is acutely aware of the mind and intelligence of God by taking notice of the communication that, for the mystic, is embedded in the rhythms (or repetitions and patterns) that are present in being. These rhythms, for the mystic, indicate intentionality or the agency of an intelligent conception.

This rhythm, for Thurman, is expressed in its zenith of the arrival of humans. The arrival of humans is understood as an infinite creative mind duplicating itself in a finite manner. He does not concern himself with the details of the creative act such as Leibniz's extensions or Whitehead's units of experience. It is only necessary, for Thurman, that he described what it meant for humans to be finite divisions of an infinite intelligent whole. The process that brought into existence the human being is also responsible for the phenomenon of self-awareness or self-consciousness. Through this self-consciousness, the human is able to take notice and experience existence. Through this experience of existence, some humans are able to take notice of certain repetitions of physical phenomena that are a part of existence. These repetitions are experienced as rhythms and have an intrinsic quality of beauty about them. One type of repetition is the experience of interconnectedness or community, which can be observed in all forms of existence. As the human becomes more aware of the existence of community, the desire to experience community on a more intimate level grows. According to Thurman, this is the mind of God realizing itself. This mind produces finite units from its own substance. These finite units then develop the desire for oneness. This act causes and produces consciousness, both individual and communal, in a continuous manner until oneness is realized.

NEWTON'S IDEA OF CONSCIOUSNESS

As with Thurman, Newton's works chosen for this study present a complete picture of his idea of consciousness. Although Newton did not attempt to be systematic, because his overall philosophical concepts were fluid, he adjusted his ideas as his field of observation grew. Newton used a Marxist approach to probe the meaning of consciousness which granted the opportunity to first examine the dialectic of consciousness. Newton also defined himself as a materialist, and thus was reluctant to examine society from the point of view of the inner being. He was decidedly more focused on society as a whole, which led to his dialogue about consciousness and humanity. Finally, while completing his graduate work, Newton wrote a paper titled "The Mind Is Flesh," because in the paper, Newton discusses the effects of consciousness on the individual.

Consciousness, according to Newton, was a concept that could be best understood if its meaning were examined using the philosophical method of the dialectic. Dialectics, as a method of philosophical inquiry, simply means to discuss a concept until a reasonable conclusion can be reached through seeking the truth from all possible angles. Søren Kierkegaard's statement, "The mind is flesh," serves as the premise and point of departure of his essay dedicated to the purpose of understanding how physical freedom is connected to consciousness. In this essay, Newton's method of philosophizing is not dogmatically focused on proving that his conclusion is correct to the exclusion of all others; however, he does attempt to show which conclusion is most probable.

Newton's use of the dialectic to infer the meaning and source of consciousness is a strong determinant in the line of reasoning he uses to develop a plan of action that could lead to the freedom of the black community. In using this method, he was able to see why certain understandings of consciousness did not fit the lived experience of the people. Therefore, any proposed solutions for raising the consciousness of the people arising from such understandings would be ineffective because they would have few applications in the material world in which Newton lived. Likewise, solutions for the problems in society that had no bases in the material world or did not address material concerns would also be doomed. Newton argued that seeking racial integration without addressing the underlying economic concerns was one such example of this type of false consciousness.

The motto for the Panthers was "All Power to the People." Within this statement was encapsulated the summative philosophical statement of the vision for the oppressed of the world. It was Newton's belief that if the people's development of consciousness were not hindered by the oppressor, it would come to pass naturally; however, because contradiction would always be a part of the material world, then it was the call of the revolutionary to raise the level of consciousness so that the people would not rest until it was their lived experience. His vision, on one level, was steeped in political theory. As a result of his belief that the basic state of nature for humanity was freedom, it necessarily followed that all power should be in the hands of the people. The idea of freedom carried with it the concept of equality. This is because no one, accordingly, should hinder the freedom of another. To do so would theoretically mean that all individuals were not free. Being free, then, carries with it the necessary complement of power, which in this sense can be defined as the ability to define one's pattern of life according to one's personal desires within the framework of human community.

This concept also carried with it a metaphysical aspect because Newton believed that man was the highest good and as such was the physical substance behind the ideological concept of God. In effect, when Newton created the statement, he was essentially performing the same literary feat performed by Marx and Nietzsche. To define the concept of God as an ideal and to then kill the ideal by stripping God's power and applying it to humans is to recreate humans, not in the image of God, but as gods themselves. The purpose of this inversion is twofold. The first purpose is to remove the fear factor and all justifications of why the oppressor is able to oppress. The second purpose is to make the people self-reliant by realizing that they, not God, determine their own destinies.

All of reality was material for Newton. From this premise, he began one of his lesser known essays. Whereas consciousness was not a physical phenomenon for Newton, he did consider it to be a quality stemming from the physical matter of the body, and not spiritual matter as some theories suggested. Outside of what Newton wrote specifically about consciousness, his writings demonstrate that a material conception of the universe had enormous effect on him. A closer examination suggests that it was Newton's goal to demonstrate that to use abstract control processes was to also control the individual physically. He demonstrated on several occasions that physical control had the same effect as mental control. One such demonstration of this phenomenon was the fact that he could not read when he graduated from high school. This, according to him, stemmed from his and others' rejection of an irrelevant subject matter. Although supposedly nothing was done to him physically, the irrelevant educational material became, in effect, a physical constraint. To reject these factors brought about real material effects such as underprivileged economic conditions. To accept the cause also brought real material effects shaping the perception of the individual, thus inducing the individual to view reality through a frame of reference irrelevant to his material existence.

From Newton's definition and also Thurman's definition and subsequent explication of consciousness, it can be clearly seen that others influenced their thoughts; however, their experience provides the most direct link to the foundation of their thinking. Because of the proximity of the oppressive conditions to each man's sphere of influence, each of them defined consciousness in a manner that readily supported the usage of the term in their theories of how oppressive social conditions could be eradicated. For Thurman, this called for the individual's realization that all persons are connected through their relationship to God, and consciousness is a direct result of this relationship. Therefore, it is in community that humans can achieve their purpose, which according to Thurman is also to achieve a clear vision of God. On the contrary, Newton did not regard consciousness as a quality of being connected to God, but rather as a characteristic of being human. He also believed that it is in community, and even a community of communities, where humans achieve their greatest purpose, which, for Newton, is to rid themselves of oppression. Neither man was satisfied with merely offering their definitions without identifying how they could be used to achieve the aims they put forth.

THURMAN'S USAGE OF CONSCIOUSNESS

Initially, when examining Thurman's understanding of consciousness and the aim of consciousness, it is easy to focus on the individual and the awakening moment of clarity when the individual becomes witness to the mystic vision. In doing so, the obvious inference derived from the pages of Thurman's own writings would be simply that the aim of consciousness is God. This is because when Thurman discusses the mystic's aim or desire, it is coupled with the concept that as the mystic has gained awareness or consciousness concerning God through the mystic vision, he now desires to be in the presence of God continually. However, there are many ideas in Thurman's writing which must be analyzed before properly defining the aim of consciousness as he understands it.

To thoroughly define the aim of consciousness, it is important to know where Thurman begins his ratiocination. All existence begins in the mind of God; therefore, it is of God, and it is God. Life is a part of existence and as such comes from God. Life itself is alive and it is aware that it is alive. This awareness or consciousness is of God, that is to say, God gives life consciousness. Thurman, on one level, defines consciousness as the ability to respond to experience. Accordingly, life has a memory or experience of being united with God and desires to be united again. From this desire follows the strong persistence of living entities, inclusive of humans, to be in community. Life seeks life.

There are also several key concepts that Thurman utilizes to assist in creating a mental image of the purposefulness of consciousness. The first of these concepts is actualizing or becoming. Thurman writes,

> It seems reasonable to say, then, that the "intent" of creation is that life lives by constantly seeking to realize itself in established forms, pattern, and units. Expressed in this way, it must not be thought that life is static, something that is set, fixed, determined. The key word to remember always is potential: that which has not yet to pass but which is always coming to pass.[15]

The word "potential" carries two notions within its conceptual base. It first brings to mind the idea that whatever contains potential has the power to become. Second, potential also raises the issue that if an entity has the ability to become, then it can be assumed that it is incomplete in its present form and any future forms until all potential has been expended. From this point of view, potential can be said to be a characteristic of life. It is well noted that one of the characteristics ascribed to life in the biological sciences is growth or development.

The second noteworthy concept is vision. Vision for Thurman is what creates the motivation needed to cause the various life forms to reach their potential. Specifically as it concerns the mystic, it is the vision bound in the memory that creates the necessity for the formation of a space conducive to the fulfillment of the vision. Thurman speaks of this in the following way: "The goal of the mystic, therefore, is to know God in a comprehensive sense; for God is grasped by the self or the whole self is laid hold upon by God, the vision of God is realized inclusively."[16] It is this realization that begins in the consciousness and is used to form a new perception of what existence means. Vision can also be thought of as a means of communication between the Creator and the creation. Thurman puts forth the concept of God having fellowship through the vision and also intimating, to those who are attentive, what could be. Thurman writes,

> And if I may enter into communion with such a God, then as a result of that communion, I may be exposed to the vision of his purposes. To the degree to which I respond to that vision I participate formally, deliberately, and consciously in those purposes.[17]

The vision becomes the initial conversational act issued from God to the referent. In this case, the referent is those from whom the vision is sufficiently inspiring to elicit a response. The initial response from the mystic comes in the form of focused desire to participate in that vision in a phenomenal way.

Finally, unity is also a concept that expands on the meaning found in Thurman's writings defining the aim of consciousness. Unity, for Thurman, encompassed more than humanity. Unity encompasses all of life. According to Thurman, "The literal fact of the unity of life seems to be established beyond doubt."[18] This is a significant factor in understanding the aim of consciousness. Thurman begins with this premise when he seeks to give a reason for what he considers to be the natural tendency of all life to be interdependent. The interconnectedness of life, therefore, cannot be thought of as having been initiated by material causes such as the mutual interdependence of various species. When applying Thurman's premise, it can only be explained through the notion that life is one, and fractionalization is destructive to life. So to this end, whenever life "feels" the unity is in jeopardy, life consciously seeks to maintain the unity at all cost.

Unity is immensely important to the other aforementioned concepts in that each of the other concepts finds its usefulness in the goal of unity of life and in the ultimate goal of unity with God. It is because of unity that life is able to reach full potential in all its forms. Unity becomes an end, but it is also a part of the process that allows for the cooperation between forms that gives them the ability to reach their full potential. Concerning this process, Thurman writes,

> Every expression of life is trying to experience itself. For a form to experience itself it must actualize its own unique potential. In doing so it experiences in miniature the fundamental unity out of which it comes.[19]

Until this process conveys to the consciousness of the individual life forms the understanding of the total unity of life, it continues to replicate itself. The end of this process is found in the unity of all life and in the ultimate aim of consciousness, which is God.

As the forms of life become better in tune with the vision, the aim of consciousness is expressed at higher levels. Consequently, it seems that the aim of consciousness is expressed at its highest level in the life of the mystic. As Thurman puts it,

> What is true of human life in general and of the developing of self-consciousness of man in particular, is also true of the mystic in worship. In his act of worship the mystic achieves a transcending unity.[20]

The consciousness of the mystic is affected by the vision. The response to the vision is to attempt to order the lived experience in such a way that the experience derived from the mystic encounter with God can be a permanent experience. This becomes the desired experience for the mystic. Eventually, this desired experience begins to make some mystics realize that if they are to continue living in a manner that is connected to the world, they must affect the world in such a way that the world's flaws are not a continuous distraction from the vision. The mystic does this by attempting to make those in their immediate surroundings aware or conscious of the role they play in obscuring the vision.

The mystic, in fulfilling the desired experience, becomes a changed entity. The aim has become so important that even those details that are considered a part of the process of fulfilling the aim become of great significance. Thurman goes as far to say that

> every new synthesis of the individual around a fresh goal, on whatever level of experience it may take place, is but an implied reference to the ultimate goal of human life, namely to know God, in some exhaustive and completely thoroughgoing sense.[21]

This becomes more important for the individual than whether he or she lives or dies. This concept can be compared with Newton's concept of revolutionary suicide. Thurman suggests that even if individuals never fulfill their goal in a quantitative manner, they can reach it in a qualitative manner. This is called "centering down," meaning to focus incessantly on one purpose.[22] Specifically, what makes the difference in the mystic's experience is the "realization" or consciousness of the vision.[23]

Thurman constantly brought to the fore the idea that it was necessary for this new consciousness to be shared with the outer community. "The first and most immediate obligation of the person whose life is fed by such religious experience is to seek to apply the insights derived to the problems of his daily life."[24] It is important to remember when attempting to understand the nature of the connection between consciousness and community in his writings that Thurman felt it was impossible to achieve the desired experience without an outward manifestation of the vision in the surrounding community. This type of mystic could not live in a viable way, knowing what was possible in life and not acting to help achieve it. The outer effect of this line of thought caused Thurman to live his life in a specifically public manner. As it pertained to community, Thurman felt it necessary to engage the issue of community in a myriad of ways. First, Thurman was a minister. It was specifically the minister who, as Thurman posited, had exerted a powerful influence in the black community dating back to the days of slavery.[25] Thurman used his ministerial role as an opportunity to speak to those social issues which he felt obscured the vision. He had the goal in mind of raising consciousness through sharing the vision he had achieved of what was possible.

Second, Thurman was a prolific writer whose writings are a testament to his efforts to change the consciousness of the reader by sharing his understanding of the vision. From the beginning of Thurman's scholarly development, he focused much attention on social change. In one such writing, "Mysticism and Social Change," Thurman focused on the idea of how to raise the consciousness of the greater community so that the vision could be realized. He writes,

> Social power in society as we know it is inevitable. The problem is to place dynamic and effective inner moral and external social checks upon the centers of social power. This can only be done by broadening the basis of social responsibility on the part of social control until it includes all of the individuals in society and by injecting a sense of high morality in the persons who emerge as a result of the radical alteration in the structure of social relationships which is involved.[26]

Thurman, in this passage, is referring to what happens when community is formed with no understanding of the greatness that is possible through the raising of consciousness. In the *Creative Encounter*, he locates the impetus for community in the human need for love. The concept is prominent in his writings. He believed that the individual could not actualize his full potential if there were not some investment from the community. For him, this is accomplished best through the sharing of the vision of God, which raises consciousness.

NEWTON'S USAGE OF CONSCIOUSNESS

Newton used the raising of consciousness to serve as the energy needed to create a movement of the people. His major goal was to stir the people's desire to want the vision of life he believed to be possible. His understanding of consciousness was derived from two sources that caused him to arrive at this conclusion. One source, as we have seen, was the writings of Karl Marx and his dialectical materialism. Dialectical materialism gave Newton the ability to interpret contradictions in history, noting that much of the use Marx found for his methodology was located in the historical clash of cultures. Newton explained in a speech at Boston University that although he set out to be an empiricist, the empiricism of Kant was useless when it came to interpreting history. He applied the laws of physics by saying that "in the physical world, when objects collide they are transformed."[27] In much the same way, when cultures collide, they are changed. Moreover, using materialism, Newton concluded that as the world is exclusively made from physical matter and consciousness is a characteristic of the physical properties of the matter that makes us human, when an individual's environment changes (which includes the social environment), so too does the consciousness. This was significant to Newton's ideology because he realized that the poor state of consciousness of the black community had much to do with the social conditions, which were repetitious examples of poverty and oppression. Newton was convinced that for blacks to desire something different, their consciousness had to be transformed into a usable form of energy.

It was in the writings of Freud that Newton found a way to transform consciousness into a usable form of energy. According to Newton, "One of the greatest contributions of Freud was to make people aware that they are controlled much of their lives by their unconscious."[28] Newton never defines the unconscious semantically or in a locative manner, but he does imply a specific meaning. Unconsciousness, for him, carries the meaning of unfocused knowledge of phenomenal events of existence, forming for the individual a skewed frame of reference that serves as a weapon against his best interests. This definition is opposed to the focused, intentionally known phenomenal events or existence that can be said to be a part of consciousness. For him, an individual who is either unconscious or unaware of a harmful phenomenal reality becomes complicit with it. Accordingly, he believed that becoming conscious essentially gave the individual power, which, as used here, is the ability to change events.

The demonstration of this power could be seen, according to Newton, in a committed life focused on the removal of any of the manifestations of oppression. Revolutionary suicide actually became an extension of this newly gained power stemming from the growth of consciousness. This connection hinged on the fact that the individual now realized that the desire to live became a tool of the oppressor because it developed a tandem concept, which was the fear of death in the individual. This fear of death could be used to threaten the individual, forcing the individual to choose life even under the most deplorable conditions. Newton developed this concept while in prison, serving time in solitary confinement. It was his belief that he was able to resist going insane because he was not overly attached to preserving his life. For him, it was less important to live than it was to allow others to believe they had broken his will or his ability to struggle against oppressive acts.

In the context of communal struggle, revolutionary suicide is demonstrated through the continuous revolutionary acts of the community in the face of extremely oppressive forces and the threat of death. The revolutionary community cannot be existentially threatened because it has realized that to live constantly in response to the fear of death is not to live at all. If the commitment to revolutionary suicide causes the early demise of the individual or community, then according to Newton, they will have lived a full life because they can now be said to have lived consciously, whereas the same cannot be said of the person who lived in constant fear. According to Newton, such individuals or communities never actualized their full potential.

The concept of intercommunalism, which is how the Panthers described their political stance as it pertained to the relationship between the black community and other communities nationally and internationally, provided the only means by which a conscious community could resist the imperialistic desires of the ruling circle. For a community, consciousness required that the community resist being controlled by the influence of those who had no direct interest in the their existence. As an ideology, Newton felt that consciousness was a natural outcome of an oppressed community's desire to resist oppression. This was because as the community becomes conscious, its resistance increases. As its resistance increases, the oppressive forces necessarily become more brutal so as to cause the desire for life to overtake the desire for freedom. Intercommunalism gives the oppressed community the ability to join with other oppressed communities. In doing so, the number of the oppressed grows. Moreover, the goods and services lacked by one community can now be provided by the other. Once the need for the oppressor's goods diminishes, the power of the oppressor also diminishes. Therefore, according to Newton, the full potential of a community can only be realized through the conscious effort of the community to direct its own future, which in turn presumes intercommunal cooperation.

In the grounding of their theories, both Newton and Thurman focus on consciousness as the essential element in the cause of change individually and communally. Thurman's usage of consciousness was bound to his experience of the mystic vision. This vision amounts to a glimpse of the possibilities of life when the individual, and even the community, is focused on Godly living, which essentially amounts to the creation of a supportive, loving community. For Newton, the potential for freedom lies dormant within the individual, and consequently, it is also dormant in the community while they exist in an unconscious state. When the consciousness is awakened, the potential of the desire for freedom can be realized. Unlike Thurman, Newton believed that as the world was wholly material, an awakening of consciousness was inevitable. Particles are always colliding, causing a constant state of change, which brings about a change in consciousness. The development of each man's usage of consciousness followed different lines of logic, to be sure; however, an awakening of consciousness is central to both of their overall philosophies. The theme of awakening or raising consciousness can be traced through all of the writings chosen for this study, regardless of whether it is mentioned explicitly or implicitly. In the next section, an examination of the chosen writings will be performed for the purpose of noting these explicit and implicit examples. Particular attention will be paid to the connection between the theme of awakened consciousness and their theories of community development and social transformation.

THURMAN AND COMMUNITY DEVELOPMENT/SOCIAL TRANSFORMATION

Thurman's understanding of consciousness was integral to his work in the area of community development and social transformation. From his earliest statements concerning community, he seemed to focus on the transcendent and transformative nature of consciousness. In the book *Deep River*, Thurman describes the slave community and the effect the slave preacher had on it through sermon. He is explicit in his description of how those early sermons served to galvanize the slave community behind the concept that they were not "Niggers," but, in fact, shared the same connection to God that the early Israelites had, as God's chosen people. This served a twofold purpose. First, it served the purpose of giving the slaves a means by which to rise above or transcend their current lot in life. It also served the purpose of transforming them from a slave community into children of God who were enslaved at the moment but who were standing at the ready, awaiting their God who would restore them.

In *Jesus and the Disinherited*, Thurman communicates the ability of Jesus to transform a community of blacks thousands of years removed, who until that moment had not considered what it meant for Jesus to be from a place with a similar socioeconomic status. This gave those who were believers "standing at a moment in time with their backs against the wall"[29] the ability to also aspire to live their life in a similar manner. They could now do this because they consciously realized that it had happened before. Thurman's understanding of the God experience, or what he called the Creative Encounter, caused him to believe that it was necessary for religion to infect the consciousness of the believer and create a transformative response to the experience. The believer, after the experience, was now much more fully conscious than before, as was Thurman after his mystic journey: "Nothing had changed except that now there was added a new dimension of awareness of what I had been looking at for some time but had not seen. Realization was added and that made all the difference."[30] Even the title, *The Luminous Darkness*, which alludes to the paradox of finding light within darkness, was used to cause the consciousness of the individual to transcend the meaning of the two words. Writing about how light can be found in the midst of darkness can transform the understanding of the darkest moments in life.

The idea of movement in a physical sense, which is caused by a great measurable force, can be compared with the force necessary to cause a movement or change in consciousness. The force of consciousness can be great enough to cause a physical movement of the people. It is evidenced in the writings of Thurman that he held the understanding that it was possible to cause a movement of the people through the raising or changing of consciousness:

> If a man feels that he does not belong in the way in which it is perfectly normal for other people to belong, then he develops a deep sense of insecurity. When this happens to a person, it provides the basic material for what the psychologist calls an inferiority complex. It is quite possible for a man to have no sense of personal inferiority as such, but at the same time to be dogged by a sense of social inferiority. The awareness of being a child of God tends to stabilize the ego and results in a new courage, fearlessness, and power. I have seen it happen again and again.[31]

Here, Thurman gives the example of the effect of the Christian experience on the individual; however, it is clear from further reading that he believes the same type of experience is possible in other religions. In this statement, he demonstrates the belief that it is possible to transform an individual's consciousness, and in doing so, the person is irrevocably changed for the better. He is able to make this claim because of his belief that what is essential about an individual is his consciousness, and consciousness can be transformed both from without and within.

Thurman put this precept into practice during his tenure as the pastor of the Fellowship Church for All Peoples in San Francisco. For Thurman, this church was a place where people of all races, all religions, and all denominations could come together in one place, at one time, and in one service sharing the worship experience. This idea stemmed from a consciousness-changing moment Thurman experienced at the Khyber Pass while visiting India. He was moved by the experience of witnessing many different races, nationalities, and faith conducting trade without incident. He posed the rhetorical question to himself, "why could this not happen in the church?" The answer came in his realization that if the way worship was perceived could be changed, then this type of experience would be possible. So then, for Thurman, to change the consciousness is not to change the environment, but rather to change the perception (or the aesthetic experience) of the environment. Accordingly, he believed that doing so would cause a change in the individual and movement in the wider community.

Although communal consciousness development was a major part of what Howard Thurman considered his life's work, initially he questioned if it were possible across racial and religious lines. As far as he was concerned, the question was already answered intra-racially, but because of the racial strife that existed within his milieu, he was not sure whether the same thing could be done in a different context. The necessity for Thurman to prove that this was possible was driven by his belief that life is one. Thurman's acceptance of the possibility was based on what he saw in his community. He speaks of the phenomena leading to the change of consciousness in *Deep River and The Negro Spiritual Speaks of Life and Death*:

> Religion was a source of consolation that had power to raise endurance to a scintillating quality. It supplied a social milieu in which

the lyric words were cast. Here we are not dealing with a philosophy of unyielding despair, but a clear sharing by the members of the group with each other of the comfort and strength each found in his religious commitment.[32]

Conscious community was witnessed in the songs that the slaves sung. It was in the sharing of comfort and strength in which the community engaged. It could even be witnessed in the common desire for freedom that bound all, young or old, into a common consciousness. How this would carry over intra-culturally could not be determined without an actual attempt, despite all the successful evidence.

The attempt to raise the consciousness of those who worshipped at the Fellowship Church could be witnessed in many ways, but most provocatively in the fact that the church made great strides in its attempt to not just be a place of worship but also a site of community transformation. One of the goals of the Fellowship Church was to provide the tools with which people might make better decisions that would enable them to apply, away from the Fellowship, the insights that were discovered there. Many organizations have claimed a similar mission statement in more recent times, but what is amazing about this one is that it came to maturity during the 1940s.

NEWTON AND COMMUNITY DEVELOPMENT/SOCIAL TRANSFORMATION

Freedom, for Newton, was an impossibility without consciousness. Newton believed that existence was constantly in a state of flux. This was because bodies, whether subatomic particles or human beings, were constantly colliding, and as a result becoming. The finer points of his philosophy began with his explanation of the nature of acculturation, which takes place after the collision of cultures. Newton did not explain his implied belief that the more dominant culture attempts to assimilate the less dominant culture. He also neglected to explain his understanding that there are a number of forces derived from a number of causes such as the force created by great numbers of bodies moving in one direction. There was also the force created by the energy of consciousness that stirs the desire to be free. It was inferred by Newton that the force created by consciousness could contend and often resist assimilation if the consciousness were sufficiently raised.

Thus, the individual possessing heightened consciousness has the weapon of awareness, which, according to Newton, enables him to fight against destructive forces.

For Newton, consciousness also serves as a cause of social movements. His terse summation of his philosophy of movement states, "If the party does not make the people aware of the tools and methods of liberation, there will be no means by which the people can mobilize."[33] He tested his premise in the creation of the Black Panther Party. He was insistent that the only purpose of the Panthers was to raise the consciousness of the people. It was his premise that the community cannot move forward intentionally without a broadly shared consciousness. Without this shared consciousness, there merely would be a rebellion without the potential for sustained change of a genuine revolution.[34]

The Panthers, under Newton's direction, engaged in the process of raising consciousness with the goal of revolution. He writes,

> The main function of the party is to awaken the people and teach them the strategic method of resisting a power structure which is prepared not only to combat with massive brutality the people's resistance but to annihilate totally the black population.[35]

The ability of consciousness to generate a political movement, according to Newton, was due to the fact that the process of becoming conscious brought to the fore those repressive elements in society that were the cause of the dialectical contradictions in society. Once these elements were identified, movement would begin. Another burst of transformative energy was sparked by the explication of this revolutionary vision within the community. As stated earlier, this stirring of the visionary desire builds the potential of the vision to become reality. One important way it did so was through the creation of survival service programs for the community. These programs were developed with the goal of allowing the people to have the opportunity to meet their needs through institutions in their own community. Consequently, the people could better organize politically because they could see the interdependence and reliability of each individual.[36]

Although it was the stated purpose of Newton and the Panthers to raise the consciousness of the people, to prove Newton's theories were possible, they had to become reality. What is unique about Newton and the Panthers was that there was never a stated goal to "Pantherize" the community. Newton seemed to believe that once the community became conscious, there would no longer be a need for the Panthers. The effect that this mode of thinking had on communal consciousness development is that it allowed the Panthers to objectify themselves to emotionally arouse the people but at the same time keep the people out of harm's way. Many of the Panthers even paid the highest cost of all in order that the image of hatred demonstrated by the oppressor could be seen in its fullest light. This can be identified in several statements made by the Panthers, such as follows:

> The party must exist aboveground as long as the dog power structure will allow, and, hopefully, when the party is forced to go underground, the party's message will already have been put across to the people.[37]

> The people make revolution; the oppressors, by their brutal actions, cause resistance by the people. The vanguard party only teaches the correct methods of resistance.[38]

> We did not expect such a repressive government to stand idly by while the Black Panther Party went forward to the goal of serving the people. We expected repression. We knew as a revolutionary vanguard, repression would be the reaction of our oppressors, but we recognize that the task of the revolutionist is difficult and his life is short. We were prepared then, as we are now, to give our all in the interest of oppressed people.[39]

The self-objectification of the Panthers was intentional. The demonstration of repression shown against the Panthers was believed by Newton to raise the consciousness of the black community, allowing them to see themselves in the Panthers and identify with their suffering. This identification by the black community would cause the community to realize that revolution was necessary. And of course, the entire Panther Philosophy was based on the assumption that deep inside, the people desired freedom.

CONCLUDING INFERENCES

Howard Washington Thurman and Huey Percy Newton were two African American men who were born during the modern era of black existence in America. They were both intellectuals who consumed much of the active scholarly period of their lives with the subject of how to improve human existence. In doing so, they used their own life experience as the basis from which to develop their ideas about correcting the problem of oppression. Each man had a vision of what society could be, particularly in the black community, unhindered by the restriction of what it meant to be black in America. This is expressed in both men's description of their lived experience, in contrast to their vision or desired experience. They describe the effects of society's oppression as the catalyst for the community's attempt to actualize its full potential. Thurman and Newton both subscribed to the belief that in order for there to be a transformation in the lifestyle of blacks, there would need to be a shift in consciousness so that blacks could transcend the ill effects of living in a society that may have tolerated blacks, but never embraced their humanity. Thurman spoke of black people as having a "cheap self estimate."[40] Newton wrote that the word "black" had become "pejorative in every sense in the American language."[41] This negative aesthetic or perception, according to each man, infected the consciousness of blacks, causing each black individually to approach society through this frame of reference. For this reason, both men and other black social thinkers of the modern era felt that consciousness was the primary concern when working for the forward progression of the black community.

Thurman's definition of consciousness grows from his mystical understanding of the universe. He subscribes to the idea that God is, and all that God is, causes all that is to be.[42] There are several clues to Thurman's understanding in his writings. Thurman, according to Carlyle Fielding Stewart, affirms the idea that God is the source of all life. God's presence may be envisioned in the smallest insect or the most majestic mountain. God is not only the source of life, as a sustainer or spiritual substance that pulls together all living matter and gives it its being, but God is also the creator of life. It is God who is the creative mind in which all living things find meaning, and because of God, living things seem to have direction and aesthetic. Thurman writes, "Thus God is thought of as the Creator. From this point of view, time-space manifestations of substance, in short, all things, even existence itself are regarded as the Mind of God coming to itself in time and space."[43] From Thurman's ideas, it can be said, however anthropomorphically, that God took part of God's being to create and quicken together the universe. It is the desire of the God substance to know itself and to be united as one. The God substance has actualizing potential as a characteristic of its essence but the desire to be united, or as Thurman purports, to be in community develops into the ability to be conscious. Thus, according to Victor Anderson, Thurman's idea of consciousness is evolutionary. Anderson writes that Thurman regards consciousness as essentially a motive and a product of community.[44] Thurman uses this understanding to explain atomic relationships, ecological balance, and even the communal grouping of living organisms; however, Thurman quickly aims this understanding toward discerning the beneficial effects of forming a human community. This theory carries within it two important points. Community becomes the object of an intentionally conscious act. From this intentional conscious act, the individual's consciousness evolves by communal focus on a single end and forms a new social reality. This means that consciousness produces community but is also heightened in community. Thurman uses a dialectical construct to explain this relationship between God and the new social reality. God, acting as thesis, creates the appetite in man for the lived experience as the antithesis. This action begins the creative encounter or mystic experience, which is the desired experience and synthesis of the latter two. The mystic experience carries the idea of group consciousness or a united social reality.

Newton's definition of consciousness develops from his dialectical understanding of existence. For Newton, existence is material. Therefore, consciousness is a function of this material existence. It is a quality of human matter such as color, shape, and smell. Consciousness, like any other quality, is affected and even determined by experience. The experience of occupying a particular space during a particular time causes the individual to express a certain manner of being. For Newton (as for Marx), the environment is the major determinant in the development and end of the individual. Moreover, individuals do not just exist in an environment—they help constitute of the environment.

Newton focused much of his attention on the conditions experienced by blacks in inner cities. Newton felt that the stress from living in such an environment caused an unconscious desire to die. Accordingly, suicide is what Newton theorized as the inevitable end for many blacks, especially black males. Newton divides suicide into two categories, reactionary and revolutionary. Reactionary suicide is defined by Newton as a desperate reaction to social conditions that the person endures, which causes the individual to develop a nihilistic worldview. In sharp contrast to reactionary suicide, revolutionary suicide focuses on the belief that life will improve only after a self-sacrificing assault on the establishment. However, neither reactionary suicide nor revolutionary suicide was a part of what constituted Newton's desired experience for blacks. Rather, Newton desired a transformative experience for blacks that could lead to freedom.

For Newton, freedom was the only desirable end for humans who had achieved the consciousness that life could be better if not for the oppression they suffered. Freedom, for Newton, was equivalent to Thurman's "living in the presence of God," because freedom was the ultimate desired end and therefore even worth dying for. From the dialectical–materialist perspective, freedom was only possible if communities of different cultures realized their interconnectedness and began to work together. Newton called this process intercommunalism. According to Newton, intercommunalism would allow all communities and the individuals in those communities to actualize their full potential. This was very similar to a social contract. Freedom would then be realized because each individual would now have worth and a responsibility to others.

For Thurman, community development was enabled by the very existence of consciousness. It followed necessarily that if consciousness were impeded, then the quality of the community would be affected. The basic principle behind Howard Thurman's concept of community is the unity of all life.[45] Accordingly, unity gives the ability to persons and nature to actualize their full potential. Once this potential is reached, persons come to recognize and realize their worth and purpose for life. Thurman's ideas follow along the lines of social contract political theorists in that he believes that consciousness is heightened in community and provides the foundation for community through shared intentionality. This experience brings about the emotion we know of as love. Love, in turn, embraces reconciliation and is facilitated by consciousness, which allows the individual to acknowledge, reflect on, and realize the presence of others. Thurman seems to have this idea in common with the Danish philosopher, Søren Kierkegaard, who believed true community was based on the individual's ability to intentionally love another.

Newton's understanding of conscious community is seen in its highest form in the Panther motto "All Power to the People." For Newton, it was the people—not the individual—which constituted the foundation of society. It was his belief that power should be held by the people or, if not, they should seize power. This understanding of community could only exist after the people had become united in an intentional revolutionary program aimed at freedom. The role of consciousness in the shaping of this type of community, according to Newton, is that a movement of the people is caused by consciousness. This movement of the people then has the ability to cause social transformation if the consciousness of the people is raised enough to understand the causes of the oppressive forces that negatively affect them. This type of community consciousness is dependent on an individual's willingness to give his life in revolutionary sacrifice for the cause of raising the consciousness of the people. The revolutionaries have their consciousness raised by being responsive to their lived experiences in such a way that they begin to deeply desire an experience beyond any experience they have known personally; yet as students of history, they believe it to be possible.

It was the intent of this research to explicate the idea of consciousness in the writings of Huey Percy Newton and Howard Washington Thurman. A secondary intent was to prove that Thurman's idea of consciousness shares common ground with Newton at the conceptual level based on their experience of being black in the oppressive reality of the African American modern era. Thurman developed and propagated an idea of consciousness oriented toward understanding the unity of all life through mystical experience. Newton developed and propagated an idea of consciousness which sought to describe the phenomenological realities of black existence through a dialectical–materialist intellectual praxis. Their concepts were unique in that they spanned the ideas of religion, philosophy of mind, metaphysics, phenomenology, and existentialism. Although Thurman was not a proponent of any one school of thought, it is clear that his ideas represented influence from several, such as Rufus Jones, Walter Rauschenbusch, and John Dewey. Newton considered himself a Marxist; however, the experiential background from which he wrote clearly identifies his writings with other black intellectuals of the modern era, such as Thurman, who focused their writings on correcting racial oppression. It was racial oppression, not economic oppression, that they felt was at the root of their specific condition. Despite the fact that Thurman was a theologian and Newton was a student of philosophy, it is apparent that there are commonalities in their writings that are much more than superficial.

The confluence that exists in their writings stems from the experience of being black during the modern era and sharing in the culture derived from the African Freedom Aesthetic. This can be identified in the concepts connecting their writings. Newton and Thurman used different sources from different schools of thought, and yet they both put forth ideas of community development based on a transformation of consciousness. The sharing of consciousness by the community was also derived by them from this aesthetic. This aesthetic was foundational to their belief in the interconnectedness of all people. The most profound nexus of confluence in their writings is the idea that the consciousness of the individual, as well as the community, has the ability to determine the physical state of the individual. They both embrace the idea that a change in consciousness gives the individual and the community the ability to transcend the problems of the lived experience. This focus also created a secondary concept in which confluence could be seen. Newton's theory of revolutionary suicide and Thurman's concept of the mystic experience of love shared the idea of the individual giving of himself as if nothing else mattered, even life itself. During a moment when many were debating the nature of consciousness, if indeed the individual could have knowledge of anything exterior to his own being, the idea of communal consciousness existing within a community is accepted by both men. Following the logic of communal consciousness, which was derived from the experiences they had as members of a communitarian culture, both Newton and Thurman put forth their own program aimed at moving the community to a higher level of consciousness.

Although each program was limited to the experiences and aesthetic perception of the individual, Newton and Thurman never attempted to separate their ideas from their culture. Both acknowledged a belief that it was necessary for the community as a whole to have a transformation of consciousness, which would in turn lead to a transcendence of the oppression that was a part of their lived experience. However unsuccessful each man was by quantitative measures, the necessary end of each man's ideas was a transformed world. Qualitatively, the success of both men can be measured only by their life's end. Newton after suffering years of harassment and incarceration at the hands of the government died in a manner that seemed to contradict his idea of revolutionary suicide. However, the alleged drug deal that took his life would only prove how difficult it is to give one's life to revolution. Thurman, however, remained committed to his path of following the religion of Jesus using spiritual disciplines. They did not transform the world, but the effect of their consciousness-raising activity advanced their communities. They advanced their communities by putting their theories into practice and focusing their labors toward community development and social transformation. Doing so allowed for the creation of movements that remained influential even after their deaths.

NOTES

1 Howard Thurman and Walter E. Fluker, *The Papers of Howard Washington Thurman* (Columbia: University of South Carolina Press, 2009), 190–222.
2 Thurman, Fluker, and Tumber, *Strange Freedom*, 108–9 (see chap. 2, n. 4).
3 Ibid., 109.
4 Thurman, *With Head and Heart*, 29 (see chap. 3, n. 2).
5 Thurman, *Search for Common Ground*, 5 (see chap. 1, n. 4).
6 Thurman, Fluker, and Tumber, *Strange Freedom*, 111 (see chap. 2, n. 4).
7 Meister Eckhart and Maurice O'C. Walshe, *Meister Eckhart: Sermons & Treatises* (Rockport: Element Books, 1992), 129.
8 Rufus Matthew Jones and Harry Emerson Fosdick, *Rufus Jones Speaks to Our Time: An Anthology* (New York: Macmillan, 1951), 11.
9 Lawrence Buell, *The American Transcendentalists: Essential Writings* (New York: Modern Library, 2006), 15.
10 Martin Heidegger and Daniel O. Dahlstrom, *Introduction to Phenomenological Research* (Bloomington: Indiana University Press, 2005), 4.
11 James Bryant and Paget Henry, "From the Pattern to Being: Howard Thurman and Africana Phenomenology," *CLR James Journal*, 12, no. 1 (Spring 2006), 61.
12 Howard Thurman, *Deep River and the Negro Spiritual Speaks of Life and Death* (Richmond: Friends United Press, 1975), 7.
13 Thurman, *Deep River*, 70 (see chap. 3, n. 22).
14 Thurman, Fluker, and Tumber, *Strange Freedom*, 109 (see chap. 2, n. 4).
15 Thurman, *Search for Common Ground*, 4 (see chap. 1, n. 4).
16 Thurman, Fluker, and Tumber, *Strange Freedom*, 109 (see chap. 2, n. 4).
17 Thurman, *Mysticism and the Experience of Love*, 11 (see chap. 3, n. 1).
18 Thurman, *Disciplines of the Spirit*, 104 (see chap. 3, n. 46).
19 Ibid.
20 Thurman, Fluker, and Tumber, *Strange Freedom*, 112 (see chap. 2, n. 4).
21 Ibid., 113.

22 "How Good to Center Down" (reading from *Meditations of the Heart*, pg. 28: 1956).

23 Thurman, *Creative Encounter*, 24 (see chap. 3, n. 34).

24 Ibid., 130.

25 Thurman, *Deep River*, 11 (see chap. 3, n. 22).

26 Thurman, Fluker, and Tumber, *Strange Freedom*, 121 (see chap. 2, n. 4).

27 Newton, Hilliard, and Weise, *Huey P. Newton Reader*, 24 (see chap. 4, n. 22).

28 Erikson and Newton, *In Search of Common Ground*, 35 (see chap. 1, n. 16).

29 Thurman, *Jesus and the Disinherited*, ii (see chap. 1, n. 24).

30 Thurman, *Creative Encounter*, 25 (see chap. 3, n. 34).

31 Thurman, *Jesus and the Disinherited*, 49–50 (see chap. 1, n. 24).

32 Thurman, *Deep River*, 27 (see chap. 3, n. 22).

33 Newton, *To Die for the People*, 15 (chap. 4, n. 17).

34 Revolution in this manner is being equated with a social movement, which focuses on political change.

35 Newton, *To Die for the People*, 15 (chap. 4, n. 17).

36 Newton, *War against the Panthers*, 30 (see chap. 4, n. 43).

37 Newton, *To Die for the People*, 16 (chap. 4, n. 17).

38 Ibid., 18

39 Ibid., 54.

40 Thurman, *With Head and Heart*, 10 (see chap. 3, n. 2).

41 Newton, *Revolutionary Suicide*, 181 (see chap. 1, n. 22).

42 Carlyle Fielding Stewart, *A Comparative Analysis of Theological-Ontological and Ethical Method in the Theologies of James Cone and Howard Thurman* (UMI: Northwestern, 1987), 137.

43 Thurman, Fluker, and Tumber, *Strange Freedom*, 105 (see chap. 2, n. 4).

44 Anderson, *Beyond Ontological Blackness*, 40 (see chap. 2, n. 32).

45 Smith, *Mystic as Prophet*, 5 (see chap. 1, n. 6).

BIBLIOGRAPHY

Adorno, Theodor W., Gretel Adorno, and Rolf Tiedemann. *Aesthetic Theory.* Minneapolis: University of Minnesota Press, 1997.

Akbar, Na'im. *Know Thyself.* Tallahassee: Mind Productions & Associates, 1999.

Anderson, Victor. *Beyond Ontological Blackness: An Essay on African American Religious and Cultural Criticism.* New York: Continuum, 1995.

Asante, Molefe K. *Afrocentricity: The Theory of Social Change.* Chicago: African American Images, 2003.

Barrett, William, and Henry David Aiken. *Philosophy in the Twentieth Century: An Anthology.* New York: Random House, 1962.

Beardsley, Monroe C. "The European Philosophers from Descartes to Nietzsche (Modern Library Classics)." Goodreads. Accessed February 28, 2012. http://www. goodreads.com/book/show/397012.The_European_Philosophers_from_Descartes_ to_Nietzsche.

Bell, Derrick A. *Faces at the Bottom of the Well: The Permanence of Racism.* New York: Basic Books, 1992.

Bloch, Ernst. *Aesthetics and Politics.* London: NLB, 1977.

Bobo, Jacqueline, Cynthia Hudley, and Claudine Michel. *The Black Studies Reader.* New York: Routledge, 2004.

Bottomore, T. B., trans. *Karl Marx.* New York: McGraw-Hill, 1964.

Brown, Sterling Allen, Arthur Paul Davis, and Ulysses Lee. *The Negro Caravan: Writings by American Negroes.* New York: Dryden Press, 1941.

Bryant, James, and Paget Henry. "From the Pattern to Being: Howard Thurman and Africana Phenomenology." *CLR James Journal* 12, no. 1 (Spring 2006): 61–84.

Buell, Lawrence. *The American Transcendentalists: Essential Writings.* New York: Modern Library, 2006.

Calhoun, Craig J. *Classical Sociological Theory.* Malden: Blackwell, 2002.

Camus, Albert. *The Rebel: An Essay on Man in Revolt.* New York: Vintage Books, 1956.

Chalmers, David John. *The Conscious Mind: In Search of a Fundamental Theory.* New York: Oxford University Press, 1996.

Chapman, Abraham. *Black Voices: An Anthology of Afro-American Literature*. New York: New American Library, 1968.

Chomsky, Noam, and Carlos Peregrín Otero. *Language and Politics*. Oakland: AK Press, 2004.

Churchland, Paul M. *Matter and Consciousness: A Contemporary Introduction to the Philosophy of Mind*. Cambridge, MA: MIT Press, 1988.

Cone, James H. *Black Theology and Black Power*. New York: Orbis, 1969.

Cone, James H. *Martin & Malcolm & America: A Dream or a Nightmare*. Maryknoll, NY: Orbis Books, 1991.

Cone, James H. *The Spirituals and the Blues: An Interpretation*. Maryknoll, NY: Orbis Books, 1991.

Césaire, Aimé. *Discourse on Colonialism*. New York: Monthly Review Press, 1972.

Dewey, John. *Art as Experience*. New York: Putnam, 1958.

Dewey, John. *How We Think*. [s.l.]: Kessinger, 2004.

Dewey, John. *The Public and Its Problems: An Essay in Political Inquiry*. Cleveland: Ohio University Press, 1991.

Dewey, John, and John J. McDermott. *The Philosophy of John Dewey: Vol. 1, The Structure of Experience. Vol. 2, The Lived Experience; [two Volumes in One]*. Chicago [u.a.]: Univ. of Chicago Press, 1981.

Du Bois, W. E. B., *The Souls of Black Folk: And Related Readings*. Evanston: McDougal Littell, 1998.

Durant, Will, and Ariel Durant. *Rousseau and Revolution: A History of Civilization in France, England, and Germany from 1756, and in the Remainder of Europe from 1715 to 1789*. New York: Simon & Schuster, 1967.

Eckhart, and Maurice O'C. Walshe. *Meister Eckhart: Sermons & Treatises*. Rockport: Element Books, 1992.

Erikson, Erik H., and Huey P. Newton. *In Search of Common Ground: Conversations with Erik H. Erikson and Huey P. Newton*. New York: Norton, 1973.

Eze, Emmanuel Chukwudi. *African Philosophy: An Anthology*. Malden: Blackwell, 1998.

Eze, Emmanuel Chukwudi. *Race and the Enlightenment*. Malden: Blackwell, 2000.

Fanon, Frantz. *Black Skin, White Mask*. New York: Grove Press, 1967.

Fanon, Frantz. *The Wretched of the Earth*. New York: Grove Press, 2004.

Felder, Cain Hope. *Stony the Road We Trod: African American Biblical Interpretation*. Minneapolis: Fortress Press, 1991.

Fluker, Walter E. *Ethical Leadership: The Quest for Character, Civility, and Community*. Minneapolis: Fortress Press, 2009.

Fluker, Walter E. *They Looked for a City: A Comparative Analysis of the Ideal of Community in the Thought of Howard Thurman and Martin Luther King, Jr*. Lanham: University Press of America, 1989.

Foner, Philip Sheldon. *The Black Panthers Speak*. New York: Da Capo Press, 1995.

Gadamer, Hans-Georg. *Philosophical Hermeneutics*. Berkeley: University of California Press, 1976.

Gadamer, Hans-Georg, and P. Christopher Smith. *Hegel's Dialectic: Five Hermeneutical Studies*. New Haven: Yale University Press, 1976.

Gadamer, Hans-Georg, and Joel Weinsheimer. *Truth and Method*. London: Continuum, 2006.

Gates, Henry Louis. *The Signifying Monkey: A Theory of Afro-American Literary Criticism*. New York: Oxford University Press, 1988.

Gay, Peter, and Sigmund Freud. *Freud: A Life for Our Time*. London: Dent, 1988.

Genovese, Eugene D. *Roll, Jordan, Roll: The World the Slaves Made*. New York: Pantheon Books, 1974.

Giddings, Paula. *When and Where I Enter*. Toronto, ON: Bantam Books, 1985.

Goatley, David Emmanuel. *Were You There?: Godforsakenness in Slave Religion*. Maryknoll, NY: Orbis Books, 1996.

Gomez, Michael Angelo. *Reversing Sail: A History of the African Diaspora*. Cambridge: Cambridge University Press, 2005.

Gordon, Lewis R. *Existentia Africana: Understanding Africana Existential Thought*. New York: Routledge, 2000.

Gordon, Lewis R. *An Introduction to Africana Philosophy*. Cambridge: Cambridge University Press, 2008.

Gyekye, Kwame. *The Unexamined Life: Philosophy and the African Experience*. Accra: Ghana Universities Press, 1988.

Hall, David L. *The Civilization of Experience: A Whiteheadian Theory of Culture*. New York: Fordham University Press, 1973.

Harding, Vincent. *There Is a River: The Black Struggle for Freedom in America*. New York: Vintage Books, 1983.

Harris, Joseph E., Alusine Jalloh, and Stephen E. Maizlish. *The African Diaspora*. College Station: Published for the University of Texas at Arlington by Texas A&M University Press, 1996.

Heidegger, Martin. *Being and Time*. Albany: State University of New York Press, 1996.

Heidegger, Martin, and Daniel O. Dahlstrom. *Introduction to Phenomenological Research*. Bloomington: Indiana University Press, 2005.

Hilliard, David, ed., *The Black Panther: Intercommunal News Service, 1967-1980*. New York: Atria Books, 2007.

Hilliard, David, Keith Zimmerman, and Kent Zimmerman. *Huey: Spirit of the Panther*. New York, NY: Thunder's Mouth Press, 2006.

Hofstadter, Albert, and Richard Francis Kuhns. *Philosophies of Art and Beauty: Selected Readings in Aesthetics from Plato to Heidegger*. Chicago: University of Chicago Press, 1976.

Hofstadter, Douglas R., and Daniel C. Dennett. *The Mind's I*. Harmondsworth: Penguin Books, 1981.

Hughey, Matthew W. "The Pedagogy of Huey P. Newton." *Journal of Black Studies* 38, no. 2 (2007): 209–31. Accessed April 11, 2012. http://jbs.sagepub.com/content/38/2/209. abstract?cited-by=yes.

Hunt, C. Anthony. *Blessed Are the Peacemakers: A Theological Analysis of the Thought of Howard Thurman and Martin Luther King, Jr.* Lima, OH: Wyndam Hall Press, 2005.

Jackson, George. *Soledad Brother: The Prison Letters of George Jackson*. New York: Coward-McCann, 1970.

Jahn, Janheinz. *Muntu: An Outline of the New African Culture*. New York: Grove Press, 1961.

Jaynes, Julian. *The Origin of Consciousness in the Breakdown of the Bicameral Mind*. Boston: Houghton Mifflin, 1976.

Jeffries, J. L. *Huey P. Newton: The Radical Theorist*. Jackson: University Press of Mississippi, 2002.

Johnson, Charles. *Being & Race: Black Writing since 1970*. Bloomington: Indiana University Press, 1988.

Jones, Charles E. *The Black Panther Party (Reconsidered)*. Baltimore: Black Classic Press, 1998.

Jones, Rufus Matthew, and Harry Emerson Fosdick. *Rufus Jones Speaks to Our Time: An Anthology:* New York: Macmillan, 1951.

Jung, C. G., and Anthony Storr. *The Essential Jung: Selected Writings*. Princeton: Princeton University Press, 1999.

Kempny, Marian, and Aldona Jawłowska. *Identity in Transformation: Postmodernity, Postcommunism, and Globalization*. Westport: Praeger, 2002.

Lawler, Mary. *Marcus Garvey*. New York: Chelsea House, 1988.

Levine, Lawrence W. *Black Culture and Black Consciousness Afro-American Folk Thought from Slavery to Freedom*. Oxford: Oxford University Press, 2007.

Levinson, Jerrold. *The Oxford Handbook of Aesthetics*. Oxford: Oxford University Press, 2003.

Lincoln, C. Eric, and Lawrence H. Mamiya. *The Black Church in the African-American Experience*. Durham: Duke University Press, 1990.

Locke, Alain LeRoy. *The New Negro*. New York: Simon & Schuster, 1997.

Manning, George, Kent Curtis, and Steve McMillen. *Building Community: The Human Side of Work*. Cincinnati: Thomson Executive Press, 1996.

Marek, Franz. *Philosophy of World Revolution: A Contribution to an Anthology of Theories of Revolution*. New York: International Publishers, 1969.

McCartney, John T. *Black Power Ideologies: An Essay in African-American Political Thought*. Philadelphia: Temple University Press, 1992.

McWhorter, John H. *Authentically Black: Essays for the Black Silent Majority*. New York: Gotham Books, 2003.

Melville, Herskovits J. *The Myth of the Negro Past*. Boston: Beacon Press, 1990.

Mitchell, Mozella G. *Spiritual Dynamics of Howard Thurman's Theology*. Bristol, IN: Wyndham Hall Press, 1985.

Napier, Winston. *African American Literary Theory: A Reader*. New York: New York University Press, 2000.

Neal, Mark Anthony. *Soul Babies: Black Popular Culture and the Post-soul Aesthetic*. New York: Routledge, 2002.

Nelson, John S., Allan Megill, and Deirdre N. McCloskey. *The Rhetoric of the Human Sciences: Language and Argument in Scholarship and Public Affairs*. Madison: University of Wisconsin Press, 1987.

Newton, Huey P. *Revolutionary Suicide*. New York: Harcourt Brace Jovanovich, 1973.

Newton, Huey P. *To Die for the People: The Writings of Huey P. Newton*. New York: Random House, 1972.

Newton, Huey P. *War against the Panthers: A Study of Repression in America.* New York: Harlem River Press, 1996.

Newton, Huey P., David Hilliard, and Donald Weiss. *The Huey P. Newton Reader.* New York: Seven Stories Press, 2002.

Nobles, Wade W. *Seeking the Sakhu: Foundational Writings for an African Psychology.* Chicago: Third World Press, 2006.

Patton, Sharon F. *African-American Art.* Oxford: Oxford University Press, 1998.

Pollard, Alton B. *Mysticism and Social Change: The Social Witness of Howard Thurman.* New York: Peter Lang, 1992.

Rosen, Stanley. *The Philosopher's Handbook: Essential Readings from Plato to Kant.* New York: Random House Reference, 2003.

Russell, Bertrand. *The Problems of Philosophy.* New York: Oxford University Press, 1959.

Ryle, Gilbert. *The Concept of Mind.* London: Hutchinson's University Library, 1949.

Sartre, Jean-Paul, and Hazel Estella Barnes. *Being and Nothingness.* New York: Washington Square Press, 1992.

Seale, Bobby. *Seize the Time: The Story of the Black Panther Party and Huey P. Newton.* New York: Random House, 1970.

Searle, John R., Daniel Clement Dennett, and David John Chalmers. *The Mystery of Consciousness.* New York: New York Review of Books, 1997.

Shelby, Tommie. *We Who Are Dark: The Philosophical Foundations of Black Solidarity.* Cambridge, MA: Belknap Press of Harvard University Press, 2005.

Smith, Luther E. *Howard Thurman: The Mystic as Prophet.* Washington, D.C.: University Press of America, 1981.

Solomon, Robert C. *From Hegel to Existentialism.* New York: Oxford University Press, 1987.

Spragens, Thomas A. *Understanding Political Theory.* New York: St. Martin's Press, 1976.

Strauss, Leo. *What Is Political Philosophy: And Other Studies.* London: Collier-Macmillan, 1968.

Thompson, Robert Farris. *Flash of the Spirit: African and Afro-American Art and Philosophy.* New York: Random House, 1983.

Thurman, Howard. *Deep River and the Negro Spiritual Speaks of Life and Death.* Richmond: Friends United Press, 1975.

Thurman, Howard. *The Creative Encounter: An Interpretation of Religion and the Social Witness.* New York: Harper, 1954.

Thurman, Howard. *Deep Is the Hunger: Meditations for Apostles of Sensitiveness.* New York: Harper & Brothers, 1951.

Thurman, Howard. *Disciplines of the Spirit.* New York: Harper & Row, 1963.

Thurman, Howard. *Footprints of a Dream: The Story of the Church for the Fellowship of All Peoples.* New York: Harper, 1959.

Thurman, Howard. *Jesus and the Disinherited.* New York: Abingdon-Cokesbury Press, 1949.

Thurman, Howard. *The Luminous Darkness: A Personal Interpretation of the Anatomy of Segregation and the Ground of Hope.* New York: Harper & Row, 1965.

Thurman, Howard. *Mysticism and the Experience of Love.* Wallingford, PA: Pendle Hill, 1961.

Thurman, Howard. *The Search for Common Ground: An Inquiry into the Basis of Man's Experience of Community*. New York: Harper & Row, 1971.

Thurman, Howard W. "How Good It Is to Center Down." Readings from *Meditations of the Heart*, 1965.

Thurman, Howard. *With Head and Heart: The Autobiography of Howard Thurman*. San Diego: Harcourt Brace Jovanovich, 1981.

Thurman, Howard, and Walter E. Fluker. *The Papers of Howard Washington Thurman*. Columbia: University of South Carolina Press, 2009.

Thurman, Howard, and Luther E. Smith. *Howard Thurman: Essential Writings*. Maryknoll, NY: Orbis Books, 2006.

Thurman, Howard, Walter E. Fluker, and Catherine Tumber. *A Strange Freedom: The Best of Howard Thurman on Religious Experience and Public Life*. Boston: Beacon Press, 1998.

Trivers, Robert. *Natural Selection and Social Theory: Selected Papers of Robert L. Trivers*. New York: Oxford University Press, 2002.

Vincent, Theodore G. *Black Power and the Garvey Movement*. Berkeley: Ramparts Press, 1971.

Walker, Evan Harris. *The Physics of Consciousness: The Quantum Minds and the Meaning of Life*. Cambridge, MA: Perseus Books, 2000.

Welsh-Asante, Kariamu. *The African Aesthetic: Keeper of the Traditions*. Westport: Greenwood Press, 1993.

West, Cornel. *Prophesy Deliverance!: An Afro-American Revolutionary Christianity*. Philadelphia: Westminster Press, 1982.

Whitehead, Alfred North, David Ray Griffin, and Donald W. Sherburne. *Process and Reality: An Essay in Cosmology*. New York: Free Press, 1978.

Wilmore, Gayraud S. *African American Religious Studies: An Interdisciplinary Anthology*. Durham: Duke University Press, 1989.

Wilmore, Gayraud S. *Black Religion and Black Radicalism: An Interpretation of the Religious History of African Americans*. Maryknoll, NY: Orbis Books, 1998.

Wilson, Amos N. *Blueprint for Black Power: A Moral, Political, and Economic Imperative for the Twenty-First Century*. New York: Afrikan World InfoSystems, 1998.

INDEX